On My Honour

Scouting - Childhood to Man
Personal Reflections

By
Mike Costello

First published by Barny Books

ISBN No: 978.1.903172.85.8

Publishers: Barny Books
Hough on the Hill
Grantham
Lincolnshire
NG32 2BB

Tel: 01400 250246
www.barnybooks.biz

Acknowledgements

I wish to thank the following:

To the writer Stephen Wade – for all his encouragement in helping me get the project off the ground

To my Wife, Mary and daughter, Edel for all the support that they have given me over the years

To Anthony Kendall GSL of Old Scout Troop in Leicester for help with providing Troop archives material and photos

Also I would like to thank all the Scouters, both past and present, of the 64/74th Leicester and 28th Lincoln

Col Robert Baden Powell started the Scout Movement and is acclaimed Chief Scout of the World. He originally wrote ‘Aids to Scouting’ for use in 1899 for the military but it reached a far wider readership.

He returned to England from South Africa in 1903 and found that his book was being used by youth leaders and teachers all over the country. He wanted to prepare the boys of that time for the future duties they might be called upon to perform; to instil in them a sense of duty, honour and high morals and in 1907 he organised the first experimental camp on Brownsea Island, Poole, Dorset bringing 22 boys together from different walks of life. From this small beginning developed The World Scout Movement of today.

‘Scouting for Boys’ was published in 1908 and his message spread world wide.

Baden Powell died in 1941 and is buried in Africa within sight of Mount Kenya.

On My Honour

The Scout movement has been in existence for the last hundred years and I have been a part of it. I joined in 1955 and, although I am approaching retirement, have never really left it. It's a way of life. It isn't a hobby or a casual interest.

I grew up in Leicester, in an area called Highfields. There were a mixture of races in our street; Irish, Welsh, Scots, German, West Indians, Polish, Ghanians. Our neighbours were called Smith and they came from Jamaica.

I went to the local catholic school, the Sacred Heart. Before that, I had been at school in County Mayo, Ireland. I have very fond memories of the headmistress at the Scared Heart, Sister Colomba who belonged to the Sisters of St. Joseph, a teaching order. I had to pass the convent on the way to school each morning and I would often wait and escort her and Sister Jemma who also taught at the school.

I joined the local Scout group when I was 12, the 64th Leicester Sacred Heart Inner City troop. I didn't consciously think that I wanted to be a scout but some of my friends were and they told me about the good things that they were doing and suggested that I went along with them. It was one of the best things that I have ever done in my life.

My proudest moment was the day I was invested. I had been a tenderfoot for several weeks and now I was to become a fully fledged scout. I must have been the happiest boy in the world as I was escorted back to the Fox patrol having taken my oath and been presented with the maroon and white kerchief of the troop and realising that now, I really was a scout.

It was soon after this that we started to get ready for the annual camp. It was to be held at Exton Hall, the home of Lord Gainsborough, near Oakham in Rutland. I didn't know what to expect but I know I shared the other boys' excitement. On the big day, Smith's Haulage lorry arrived to take us.

The tents, equipment and luggage was loaded first and then we sat on top of it. Smith's lorries always took us camping and it was a real experience with the wind ruffling our hair and making it difficult to talk. If it rained, we simply had a tarpaulin sheet pulled over us.

My first Summer Camp at Exton Hall in 1955.
Scouts from left: Spider Aston, author in the middle and Brian Slavin nearest the camera.

I can still remember the feeling of anticipation and excitement with which we arrived at the camp site. To us city dwellers, it was like our idea of heaven. The lorry had to be unloaded and the tents and dining shelters had to be put up first. The kitchen area was roped off. The grease and fire places had to be dug out. Camp gadgets like the wash bowl stands and the plate racks had to be put in place. There was one task that nobody was keen to undertake and that was the digging out of the latrines. (There were no Elsan or chemical toilets in those days). A waste pit had to be dug and the area was enclosed with Hessian sacking so you did get some privacy except on the occasion when the wind blew it away. The toilet seat was a couple of poles with a cross piece lashed to them on which you perched. It was hard luck if you weren't good at balancing. One lad lost his balance when it was half full and fell right into the cess pit, right up to his thighs. One of the leaders had to hose him down before any of us would go near him.

Once the tents were erected and we had eaten our lunch, we changed out of our uniforms and into our camp dress. We made sure our uniforms were hung up on a spider, a kind of special hanger. The next task was to get our patrol jobs done such as building a flag pole, setting up first aid facilities, laying out the kitchen area and, the most important job of all, erecting the grub tent. A task rota was set up for the following two weeks, fire lighting, water carrying as well as seeing to the tidiness and cleanliness of our own tent and surroundings.

Swift Patrol

Falcon Patrol 1962

Care was always taken not to put rookies together when the rota was made otherwise you were likely to get a burnt supper. At the end of each day, we collected in the marquee for our supper, a slab of fruit cake and a mug of steaming hot cocoa. Prayers were then said and, as soon as they were finished, we retired to bed. Preparing for bed was an ordeal, especially on the first night. Changing into pyjamas and laying out your bed roll in a cramped position of the tent with seven other boys sharing it wasn't easy. The tent had to be properly secured to make sure that if it rained in the night, you and your gear wouldn't get wet or, and it happened to us, you didn't roll out of the tent and finish up in the middle of the field. Another task was to hammer down all the bumps in the ground with a mallet, or at least in the area where you intended to sleep, if you wanted to wake up the next morning without a stiff neck. All these things had to be completed within half an hour because that was when the scouter came round for lights out. None of us ever slept very well the first night. We were too excited and boys tended to roll out of their sleeping bags and often finished up in a heap in the middle of the tent. And our patrol leader snored like a pig. We would have to keep digging him in the ribs or try to make him change his position.

Breakfast at camp was good; eggs, sausages, bacon, beans. Then we would have to get everything tidy for the daily inspection

The main thing that remains in my mind about that first camp was the level of comradeship that I experienced. It was to stay with me throughout my highs and lows in life and throughout my scouting career. The other thing that has stayed with me is the sheer peace and beauty of the English countryside and Lord Gainsborough's family that let us camp on their land. The two daughters were very interested in what we were doing and used to ride down on their horses to talk to us.

The next milestone for me was when I was made an assistant patrol leader. I was 13. I had to back up the patrol leader and cover for him when he was away and it wasn't always easy. Some of the boys were exuberant and didn't always like being told what to do. The experience stood me in good stead when, later on, I became a Scout leader and ran my own troop.

The soapbox Derby was a big event in Scouts and we spent weeks getting ready for it. We scoured the streets for old pram wheels, lengths of wood, boxes, old bikes, anything that we could use to build a pedal cart for the annual Derby. It was going to be run at Tollerton Airfield in Nottinghamshire. Ours looked superb when it was finished. It was called 'Heartbreak' and it had cost us £2.19 shillings in old money to build. It was silver in colour and had a top speed of 22 m.p.h. on the flat. We ironed out all the teething problems in the streets round our H.Q. We were all very proud of our car. 'Tollerton today,' we thought, 'Brands Hatch tomorrow.' On the big day, our car lived up to its name. We did well in the initial cub and scout races but, when it came to the senior scouts, our driver, Morgan McAlinden, crashed. The car was a virtual write off. Spirits were low but we comforted ourselves that there was always another year. However there never was.

The summer camp in 1956 was held at Penmaehmawr in North Wales and it rained. It rained night and day. We had to dig trenches round the tents to drain off the water and we had to keep on checking that our tent was storm pitched and brailed properly. (Storm pitched means crossing the guys diagonally over the sides of the tent to keep it down in high wind. Being brailed is to ensure the sides of the tent and the doors are pegged down tightly.) Despite our best efforts, clothes and bedding were soaked and we had to spend the rest of the first week sleeping in the farmer's barn and drying out our clothes. The biggest laugh of the week was when I was butted on my behind by a ram who had taken exception to our being there. The farmer had forgotten to tell us that he was in the barn. However no serious damage was done, except to my dignity. We spent most of our time doing badge work and getting patrol log books up to date.

The following week turned out to be a scorcher. Our dampened spirits quickly recovered and we went trail laying, gadget making, backwoods cooking and bivouacking. One of our patrol, Joe Scott, tripped over a guy rope and broke his arm but he refused to go home and spent the rest of the camp with his arm in a sling.

1957 started with a new patrol being formed, the Otter Patrol and I was made its first patrol leader. Our Scout leader was Skip Everitt and the brothers, Jim and Kim McAlinden were assistant leaders. We also had Cyril Harris and Dr Cloggy who used to come to camp with us and also joined us for other activities. The cub leader, Arkela Harry Brown always came camping with us in the summer. He was a bachelor from Wigston and we composed a song in his honour.

Do not trust him gentle maiden
For his name is Harry Brown.
Do not trust him gentle maiden
For he comes from Wigston Town.

He was a darling man but that did not prevent him from moaning about the food. He was always complaining about it. At one camp, he complained that the main course was cold but the pudding that day was hot rice and some of it fell through the gaps in the table and fell on his bare knees. Arkela jumped up with a roar of pain, dancing around and using a foreign language that was not fit for our tender ears. At the same time he was performing some kind of tribal war dance. Our laughter didn't help. The next day we had curry which was a bit too hot for Arkela and he grabbed the water bottle and took a swig of what he thought was water. It wasn't. It was white vinegar which one of the cooks had accidentally left on the table. Arkela never complained about the food being cold again.

From L-R:
Q, Skip, Bosun,
Cyril with
Arkela at the
front. 1956

I attended numerous Whitsun and Easter District Patrol camps between 1957 and 1962, mainly around the Leicestershire area. Our main district camping site was at John Lees woods which most of the scouts called John Fleas wood on account of all the midges. Other camp-sites were at Seagrave, Ratclife, Slewston and Oaks in Charnwood.

I have the fondest memories of camping at Seagrave with the senior scouts and loading all our gear on to the trek cart. We pushed and pulled it several miles to the camp site. On one occasion, a wheel came off and the cart careered down a hill and ended up in a ditch with our belongings being scattered all over the place.

Our summer camps included one at County Wicklow in Ireland. We camped on Lord Powercourt's estate. This was the troop's first overseas camp and we were limited as to how much gear we could take. While we were waiting at Liverpool to board the boat to Dublin, Skip and myself went for a walk. We were approached by an American lady who had told us that when her father knew she was visiting Britain, had told her that she was to give an Uncle Sam slide (woggle) to the first two English scouts that she met and we were the two. I've still got mine.

There are two things that stick in my mind about that camp besides the beautiful estate with its delightful gardens and hundreds of acres of countryside. The first was standing on top of Sugar Loaf mountain looking at the breath-taking views around us and the second was our trip to the Players cigarette factory in Dublin.

Sugar Loaf Mountains, Ireland in 1958
From L-R: Stag Steel, Spider Aston & Author

Following an interesting trip round the factory and a pleasant tea afterwards, we were all presented with a souvenir, a tin of twelve cigarettes. We all looked at Skip to see if he would say anything. Three of us were fifteen and the rest were all between the ages of 11 and 14. Skip was a smoker himself and he didn't seem bothered that we had been given the cigarettes so, when we got back to camp, we three older ones decided to light up. Halfway through the puffing session, we heard Skip coming and tried to stub out our fags. As soon as the tent flap was lifted, all the smoke went out through the gap. Then we got a pep talk about the dangers of smoking. I felt so sick afterwards that it was my first and my last attempt at smoking. Needless to say, I brought the rest of the cigarettes home and gave them to my uncle Jim. He smoked like a chimney.

One of the main features of a Scout's uniform is the group neckerchief or scarf. It has other uses rather than simply being worn round the neck. In an emergency, it can be used as a triangular bandage or as head cover, a sweatband or even something in which to carry your lunch. Every troop had its own distinctive colour with or without a badge or logo on the back. Ours at the 64th Sacred Heart was maroon and white.

If worn properly, the neckerchief had to be washed, ironed and starched so that it always looked clean. From the back, no more than five inches of scarf should show. Following the amalgamation with the 107th Holy Cross troop, (because of its falling numbers) we changed our scarf for a gold colour with KI-RO on the back. KI-RO was the Greek spelling for Christ.

I left school in 1958 and went to the Sea Training School in Gravesend in Kent as a catering trainee. At the end of the course, I was assigned to the P&O Company and worked on the liner the S.S.Arcadia, 30,000 tons which was then the pride of the fleet. I kept in regular contact with the scouts. Apart from a three-month world cruise, I went home every ten weeks. Our normal run was the £10 assisted scheme to Australia. Being in the merchant navy, I could have joined the Deep Sea Scouting section but I was not aware of that at the time.

Because of my naval commitments, I missed the 1959 summer camp but I was able to go the following year. We went to Alderwasley for a second time. We were getting ready to go out one day when Cloggy, one of the leaders decided to show us how clever he was at pole vaulting when the Scout Leader's back was turned by jumping over his canvas framed bed. Unfortunately he missed and fell heavily on to the bed ripping the canvas from the frame. That was serious. Skip could not sleep on the ground because he suffered from a war wound which he had sustained when he was in the navy. When Skip discovered what had happened, Cloggy was presented with needle and cotton. He had to stay behind and repair the bed while the rest of us went out.

I became an assistant Scout leader in 1961 and started to learn the ropes of being a leader rather than one of the boys. The fun and adventure element was still there although I had to deal with increased responsibilities and duties. I had to assist the Scout master and the other leaders in running the troop. The custom in the 64th was for each Scout leader to adopt a scout name rather than allow the boys to call us by our Christian names and become too familiar. Because I was in the navy, I was called Bosun. Other leaders had names like Digger (Spider Aston) as he was a keen gardener and Tracker, (Steve Mullins) who possessed good scouting skills.

At my first camp as a leader in the Isle of Man, I was given the task of Quartermaster. I was responsible for planning the menus with the patrol leaders, purchasing the food, keeping accounts of money spent, storage of food and general hygiene. Along with the sanitary engineer, the Quartermaster's job was one of the most important in the camp and was vital in keeping everyone fed and healthy. The last thing you wanted was for a tummy bug to get amongst the scouts.

I was helped by two assistants who were usually patrol leaders or assistant PLs. If my assistants did their duties well, they could gain their quartermaster's badge. My success as a Quartermaster was somewhat mixed. I dropped one or two clangers such as forgetting to order enough milk but I rather overdid it with the eggs. I bought far too many. We all ate eggs. We had eggs, eggs and more eggs in a variety of way, scrambled, boiled, poached and fried.

Isle of Man – Camp Dresser 1956/57

We had the occasional grub tent raid by the scouts but we also experienced a few we hadn't expected. Biscuits started to disappear but the biscuit thief had his preference. He only stole jammy dodgers. We had a jammy dodger thief. The biscuits were kept in a tin and, every morning, the lid was off and the biscuits gone. We were mystified. However firmly we tied the tent down or remained on watch, the jammy dodger thief would return night after night and we never caught a glimpse of him. Then the penny dropped. Hungry scouts weren't the culprits. Hungry squirrels were, squirrels with a sweet tooth. Then the eggs started to disappear and this time we caught the thieves red handed. In fact I had never seen anything so ingenious. Rats were coming in from the nearby woods and they worked in pairs. Their modus operandi was for one of them to lie on its back clasping the egg in its claws while the other caught hold of its tail and dragged it away.

It was hard work being the quartermaster and I was ready for my bed, sorry, sleeping bag. There was this night when I eased myself in and my feet touched something wet. I clambered out a lot quicker than when I went in. Somebody had put a load of wet seaweed in my sleeping bag. I never got in to it without checking it after that.

We camped at St. Ives in Cornwall in 1962. We visited Penzance and Polperro where the international telephone cable was laid but, for me, the Zennor Church took some beating. Local legend has it that the vicar of this tiny Church looking over the sea had a son with a beautiful voice. One night, the mermaids heard him singing and they enticed him away into the sea. Consequently, if you ever visit the Church, you will find a pool of water on the back pew where the mermaid sat. Sure enough, when we arrived, there was the pool of water being photographed by tourists but the coach driver told us on the way back to camp that one of the other drivers used to nip in when he saw some tourists approaching and put the water on the seat.

The other main event for me in 1962 was that I commenced my leader training with a view to gaining my Wood Badge which dictates that the holder is a trained leader. The wood badge is actually two wooden beads on a leather thong. The origins of it go back to the time when Baden Powell was serving in the army in South Africa and was presented with a necklace of bear teeth by a Zulu chief. Now wooden beads have been substituted for the teeth which you receive if you successfully complete the course. The actual wood badge training consists of two weekends after which, if you are successful, you receive the Turk's head (a leather woggle). Twelve months later, you are expected to attend a further two weekends at either the regional training centre or at Gilwell Park in Surrey, the national training centre. On completing the theoretical and practical parts of the course, you receive your coveted beads and become a member of the 1st Gilwell Scout Troop along with all the other U.K. and overseas leaders.

Author aged
19, 1962

My training course was at Ullersthorpe in Leicester at Easter 1965 when there was snow on the ground. There were 18 of us in three patrols. I was in the Pigeon patrol. We were treated like the scouts who would be in our care. We were really put through our paces taking part in activities during the day and note taking in the evening until eight or nine o'clock when we were given permission to have a drink at the local pub if we were lucky. We were given various initiatives to carry out against the clock. At each test, a different member of the patrol would act as patrol leader. My particular challenge was to get a team of six across an outdoor swimming pool on a raft. We were in full uniform and the last person across had to bring a lighted 'sacred fire' to appease the Gods. Our allocated time was 15 minutes. Anyone who fell into the pool was considered drowned and out of the exercise. The winning patrol was the one that managed to get the fire across first. I got the first two members across safely but time was running out so I decided to double up on the numbers. Unfortunately the raft developed a wobble when it was half way across the pool and the crew members were unable to rectify it. The raft turned right over and the two leaders and their equipment were deposited in the water. I was not the most popular person of the day. There was some consolation. The Pigeon patrol was the only one to get the 'sacred fire' across.

Another task was to construct a vehicle from oil drums, pole and ladders but no ropes to take us over the surface of a swamp. Anything that fell into the swamp was considered lost. We got the drums together and put the ladders on top and had patrol members stationed at the back with the poles to propel us forward and two at the front to use their poles as brakes. All went well initially until we got half way when, despite our best efforts, the oil drums started to roll in different directions and they, with the ladders and poles, ended up in one untidy heap in the middle of the swamp. The judges commented that although we had failed to achieve the objective, we had provided the biggest laugh for years.

Back, from left: Morgan, Mike. Front, from left: Skip, Arkela, Q
Oxford 1964 Summer Camp

The last objective was to construct a swinging derrick over the swimming pool and demonstrate its uses to our judge, Lord Crawshaw who was observing that day. We were given two hours to make it. We persuaded our patrol leader, Mike Wilkinson, to sit in the seat. Once we had him at our mercy, we lowered him over the swimming pool until his boots touched the water. We then roped off the derrick and left the P.L. dangling there until he promised not to give us a hard time.

This picture features the author on the left wearing an anorak with the hood up

Other parts of the training included gadget building, rope work, cooking skills, maps and compass work and hiking. In addition we looked at ceremonies and investitures, flag breaks and courts of honour.

The wood badge course was designed for leaders to experience what it was like to be a scout and to carry out the tasks we expected them to do. The course was also to hone old skills and learn new ones. The training included comradeship and working together to achieve a common aim. Scouting is meant to be an adventure that captures the enthusiasm of young people and affects their lives in a positive manner.

Kipling said, "Who hath smelt wood smoke at twilight, who hath heard the birch log burning, who is quick to read the noises of the night, let him follow with the others for the young men's feet are turning to the camps of proved desire and known delight."

I received my wood badge and certificate in September 1965. My certificate number showed, that since 1919 when Gilwell Park was presented to the Scout movement, I was the 25,156th leader to complete the wood badge training.

The other main event that year was the County camp and cub rally in July at Whatton Park near Loughborough, the home of Lord Crawshaw. We were there to welcome the new Chief Scout of Great Britain and the overseas territories, Sir Charles McClain. The other notable feature of that camp was that parents and friends came to visit us for the day. We had to butter 80 loaves of sliced bread and keep four gigantic tea-pots constantly filled up for our hungry guests. Besides meeting the Chief Scout, Sit Charles McClain, we were entertained by the Corpus Christi School pipe band. Several of our boys were in that, Michael Murphy, James Henry and Alex Stembersi. We had lads from nine different countries in our troop. We were really proud of our boys in the band.

On the first evening we were there, we had bread and soup for supper. We didn't know that the Chief Scout was wandering round the camp site and he happened to come to our corner. There was one solitary scout tending the fire and keeping an eye on the soup. The Chief got into conversation with him and asked if could have some soup. Robert had no idea who he was and he gave him some soup. Sir Charles thanked him and said how much he had enjoyed the soup to which Robert replied, "Scouts should share and share alike."

The next day at the gathering of the whole camp, the Chief related how the scout had shared his soup with him. He held this up as an example of brotherliness and hospitality. There was one red faced scout amongst our ranks and one very proud scout troop.

In the words of one of our scouts, it was a, 'glorious weekend.'

Later that year, Dr Cloggy, a former scout leader, was married at St James, Spanish Place. Other highlights were the 64th gaining 3rd place at the Leicester Scouts Swimming Gala and the senior scouts reaching the finals of the National Cooking Competition. In addition to this, 'Q' Laurie Brown gained his wood badge at Gilwell.

Calthorpe in Norfolk was the site for our summer camp in 1963. Two things stand out in my memory of this camp. On arrival, the scouts pitched their tents at one end of the field while we put ours up at the other end. In the early hours of the morning, I threw my hand out of the sleeping bag and heard a splash. Switching on my torch, I discovered shirt, shorts, socks and other things floating about in several inches of water. Waking Spider Digger Aston who was in the tent with me, we quickly scrambled outside concerned that the poor scouts would be flooded out and would need our help. When we got to their end of the field, we discovered that it was completely dry and they were all fast asleep. We slunk away to re-pitch our tent and dry out our gear.

There was a dyke running alongside the camp site and, in a moment of madness, Cyril Harris and I decided to canoe down it at midnight. We strapped lamps to the canoe and set off. We covered several miles, viewing the night life at close quarters, water voles, rats and stoats. We spent a fascinating few hours observing the activity that we would not have normally seen. Fortunately there were no mishaps and we returned safely to camp but we kept our trip secret. Skip would not have approved.

We moved into our extended head-quarters during the year. It was situated under the Parish Social Club. Thanks to the efforts of the leaders and senior scouts, 150 tons of earth was extracted from the site. Their efforts saved money. We just had to pay £50 to have it carted away. We raised a further £500 for labour costs and materials in the traditional scout manner, jumble sales, cheese and wine evenings etc.

Opening the extension by Lord Crawshaw, the County Commissioner of Leicester in 1963 From the back, L-R: Kim, George, Morgan, Digger, Author, Q, Arkela, Skip, Chill. Sitting L-R: County Commissioner, Lord Crawshaw and Mrs Botrill

The troop magazine celebrated its first anniversary in 1963.

In 1964 we went to Youlbury near Oxford for our summer camp. Unfortunately I couldn't go with the troop because I had to work until half past five. I sent all my kit on ahead and, as soon as I had finished for the day, I went home, changed into my scout uniform and set off for Oxford on my auto-cycle. The bike had a two-stroke engine and had been given to me by my boss. It was capable of travelling at 35 m.p.h. on the flat and considerably more going down hill. All went well until I reached the outskirts of Kidlington. I was going along the road quite happily and the next minute I was lying in the ditch with the bike on top of me. The lights were smashed and the bike was twisted. Clearly it was not rideable. I was covered in mud and I had a deep cut on my knee. I didn't know how long I had been lying there but it must have been for a few minutes. By the time I had staggered to my feet it was half past ten and I wasn't sure where I was.

There was a house about a hundred yards away and I made for it. I knocked on the door and a woman looked out of the bedroom window and said that she wasn't going to open the door at that time of night. I explained the situation and asked if I could leave my bike there and collect it on the way home in two weeks time. I am sure the lady was frightened by my dishevelled appearance but she told me to take the bike round the back and put it in the outhouse. Then she told me I was two miles from Kidlington.

I spotted a policeman as I reached the outskirts of the small town and asked him where I could find overnight accommodation. He directed me to a pub at the other end of the village. On I trudged. I had the pub in my sight when someone tapped me on the shoulder and a man introduced himself as the local scout leader. He said that he and his wife had seen me enter the village and realised that I was in need of help. He took me back to his house and his wife bathed my wounds and put me up for the night. I was given breakfast the next morning and pointed in the right direction. My host refused to accept any money. There was no doubt that my guardian angel was looking down on me that night.

I set off at a steady pace. I was still wearing my scout uniform. I hadn't gone more than a mile when a young man on a motor cycle gave me a lift for five miles. Then I got a lift in a van for a few miles. No sooner had I started walking again when an R.A.F. officer stopped and gave me a lift right to the camp site entrance. I think I was offered the lifts because I was in scout uniform. Scouting was held in high esteem in those days. It's not always the case today.

The main event of that camp happened when we were returning from a swimming session in Oxford. We had to go down a long lane with large houses on one side to reach the camp. A senior citizen was burning garden rubbish when the fire got out of hand and set fire to his fence and was creeping towards his house. The first scouts to reach the lane heard the old man's cries and dashed into the garden.

They started beating the flames out with anything to hand, namely wet towels and swimming trunks. Some scouts found an old stirrup pump and connected it to an outside tap and aimed the water at the heart of the fire. By the time the fire brigade arrived, the fire was under control. The Fire Chief personally thanked the scouts for their help. The lads were regaling each other with details of their exploits all the way back to camp. There were certainly one or two singed towels and smudged faces but there was a general feeling that the scouts had acquitted themselves well.

This year saw the holding of the Grand Reunion and Anniversary dinner in November to celebrate the 30 years of the 64th Leicester Sacred Heart Scout group, 1936 – 1966. The guest of honour at the celebration was the Lord Mayor and Lady Mayoress of Leicester, Alderman A.H.A.Kimberlin and Mrs Kimberlin and our parish priest, the very Reverend Dean Murdoch. There were 140 people at the reception. A full account of the dinner with a photo appeared in the Leicester Mercury. There were so many memories and a chance to meet old friends. It was a very special occasion.

The 1965 camp was held at Kingsdown in Kent. There were many highlights. The day trip to Boulogne sticks in my memory, especially the time that we six leaders were sitting outside a street café sipping wine and eating French sticks and cheese, the lads having gone off in groups to explore the town, giving us a couple of hours respite. We must have looked French with our sunglasses shorts and tans because we were approached by a typical English family, Mum, Dad and two children. Dad had a handkerchief, knotted in four corners, tied round his head. He asked us for directions in broken French and in broken French we answered him, using a lot of gestures and rolling of the eyes, shrugging of shoulders and pointing. After a while, the penny dropped and he realised we weren't French at all and it finished up with us all laughing.

The best judge of any camp is the consumer – the Scouts. We asked them what their likes and dislikes were. The camp gallup poll findings were first the likes;- tea in the morning, sleeping, eating, days out, badge work, trip to France and comradeship. Dislikes were;- washing and drying up, inspections and tent tidying.

1966 Calthorp, Norfolk
Back row: Q, Digger, Cyril
Front row: Author, Skip, Arkela

The Advance Party Report was published in June 1966. Many changes were advocated. From October 1967, scouts were to wear long trousers. Out went our khaki Melton shorts, long socks and garter tabs. Leaders also lost their distinctive beret plumes, belts and shoulder knots. Uniforms were the most tangible form of change. The A.P.R. removed the aforementioned badges and insignia and was the biggest change since we lost the big scout hats in 1957 that had been in use since scouting had started in 1907. There was a great deal of sadness in our troop, particularly among the senior scouts. Admittedly we used to be teased about our shorts, particularly by the girls.

"Who wears short shorts?" they used to call after us and we would reply, "We're not afraid of showing our legs."

The argument for the abolition of the shorts was the damaging aspect of our public image. Scouting, they thought, was dubbed a juvenile activity because of the method of dress. Criticism was also levelled at the Boer War appearance of the uniform. I have to admit that, although I was sorry to see the uniform go, some of our rather portly leaders in shorts was not a pretty sight to behold.

I joined the Senior Scouts as an assistant leader in the first half of 1966. Digger (Michael Aston) was the leader assisted by Jim McAlinden (Kim), Steve Mullins (Tracker) and Walter Stageman (Staffs). The changes recommended by the A.P.R. (Advanced Party report) were brought in to help both sections.

Skip was awarded the Medal of Merit which was presented to him at the Annual Camp Fire Festival in de Montfort Hall in Leicester. Over 90 of our group attended and we almost lifted the roof with our cheering.

My first senior camp was held at Kirby Mallory with three senior patrols – Kennedy, Scott and Wingate. Activities that were undertaken included driving lessons, Go-karting and Car-in-Trial. The only other thing I remember about that camp was ordering the food from the International Store.

The Loughborough Scouter Conference was held in Loughborough at the Ceredon School in the town. It was an annual event and had been held there since 1964. It was for Scout and Guide leaders and was a two day event. In the words of Roy Heathfield, the District Commissioner, it was to look at Scouting from both sides, in and out and, by so doing, get our sights into perspective again if we felt we had slipped a little.

The first conference I attended was in 1965. We looked at such topics as paid or voluntary leadership, games for fun, and Scouting on new housing estates. Entertainment included hand bell ringing, an indoor camp fire and a display by the Breaston Highland pipe and Drum band. Guest speakers included people from the scouting world, the Registrar of Loughborough Technical College and the Governor of Lowdham Grange Prison.

We celebrated the Diamond Jubilee of Scouting in 1967. The conference that year included sub-aqua demonstrations, public services and police training. I attended my last conference in 1979 when we looked at Outward Bound and involving our young people in outdoor activities. The Scout movement was certainly keeping abreast of the times and the needs of modern youth.

Scouting in inner city areas and other deprived communities was introduced and Scout Reach projects were started in Merseyside, Birmingham, Leeds and Warrington. Later we started one in Leicester. We also looked at activities in which groups such as Sikh, Hindu and Moslem communities could participate. We had a Sikh group in East Leicester and they looked resplendent in their green turbans.

Baden Powell had meant Scouting to be a game full of adventure, happiness and laughter. However there is a serious purpose behind these games, a basic training method that will encourage the scouts to put the two commandments into their everyday life, 'Love thy God' and 'Love thy neighbour.'

In 1950, the late Pope Pius XII said, "Experience has shown that Scouting possesses a character forming power and that the principles which it sets forth of honour, rightness, a chivalrous spirit, generous readiness to help ones neighbour are well suited to boys' nature."

Baden Powell asked those who joined the Scout movement to do their best and give first place to their duty to God.

"No boy is much good unless he has a religion," he said.

Boys, and later girls, could join whatever their colour, country, class or creed.

Scouts could either join an open group or a sponsored group. The open group is in the control of the Scout-master. The sponsored group is in the direct control of a group, a school or a Church. In our case, our sponsor was our parish priest.

I went on my first expedition with the Senior Scouts to Belgium and Luxembourg for two weeks. We had three leaders, Laurie Brown

(Q) as senior Scout leader, Eric Everitt (Skip) and myself as Assistant Senior Scout Leader. In addition there were 13 Senior Scouts divided into three patrols, Kennedy, Scott and Wingate. Among the Seniors were three Queen's Scouts (the highest award a scout can achieve).

We travelled from Leicester to Dover, across to Ostend and on to Ghent where we were met at the station by a group of Flemish scouts. They provided transport to take us to their headquarters where we stayed for the evening. After a meal, they took us to the Cathedral. They had somehow managed to get hold of the key so we had a very private viewing of this magnificent building. It was certainly an occasion to treasure. After providing a hearty breakfast for us the following morning, we attended High Mass in the Cathedral which was sung in Latin and was a very uplifting experience. After Mass, we went sight seeing, had lunch and then went to a museum. Some of the scouts played volley ball or soccer at a local school. We had an early meal at a restaurant and spent the rest of the evening exploring Ghent. We said our goodbyes after breakfast the next morning and thanked our hosts. They refused to accept a farthing for their hospitality.

We continued on our travels and, following three changes of trains, arrived at Wiltz in Luxembourg at 5.43 p.m. It was sweltering hot. We reported to the International Bureau which is the meeting place for scouts from all over the world and is actually situated in Castle Wiltz. It belongs to the scout movement.

We set up camp in the castle grounds and then tried to buy some food which we found was in very short supply because it was a religious feast day in the town. We had been restricted as to the amount of food we could take with us. Q did a wonderful job so we didn't go hungry. The next day was a free day so we wandered round the town swapping badges. The next day, three of our scouts, Mark, Jan and Tomasz went on their venture journey to Germany, a two day trip. The rest of the group went to a nearby lake and went swimming.

A couple of days later, we all went on an excursion to Germany. We caught a train to Clervaux and then hiked towards the little German town of Dasbourg. There was nearly a diplomatic incident on the German border. We'd been walking towards the border post, a distance of some 6 kilometres and we were strung out along the road. I was in my usual position of sweeper, staying at the back and making sure nobody was left behind. We reached the border post which was a striped pole across the road and a small guard room to one side. The scout leader was informed that two of the seniors had been arrested by the solitary guard and were now in the cells. It appeared that the first two lads who had arrived had sat down on the bar across the road to wait for us to catch up. Because it looked solid, they thought it was made of solid metal. Unfortunately it turned out to be light alloy and it had bent in the middle.

The guard could speak very little English and we could speak even less German. He was marching up and down in the best military fashion and looking at the bent pole while repeating 'kaput, kaput.'

Border post German/Belgian border 'Kaput' 1967

Apparently he had phoned his superior who arrived eventually and informed us in perfect English that he had been a prisoner of war in World War II in England. He told us that, although he could see the funny side of the bent pole, he thought those responsible should pay for the damage. We were happy with that decision. He fined the scouts several marks, knowing full well that we didn't have any German money and he wouldn't accept Belgian francs. He took them into the town where they changed their money at a bank. He fined them £12 each and that made a considerable hole in their spending money.

He was very affable after the fine had been paid and wished us a good holiday before he drove off and we continued on our way. As we entered the town, Q tripped over a sack of potatoes and sent them spilling all over the pavement much to the amusement of the passers by. It was even funnier as we tried to get them all back into the sack.

We had a lot of fun trying to order food, speaking in part English and part German and a great deal of sign language and face pulling.

Then when we got back to Clervaux, we discovered that we had missed the last train back to Wiltz. The train we had expected to catch wasn't running due to it being another saint's feast day. Nobody had bothered to tell us. It was put to the scouts, did they want to sleep the night in Clervaux and catch a train the next morning or have a good meal and an overnight hike back to camp, a distance of some 20 miles or so. In true scout fashion, they chose the overnight hike. I think the prospect of a good meal persuaded them. It was half past two in the morning before we got back to camp having set out at half past eight. The last few miles were painful for those who did not have the correct footwear and one or two finished up with painful blisters and had to be helped along the last couple of miles.

We all slept soundly until mid-day and when we eventually roused ourselves into motion, we discovered new tents had been erected nearby. We went across and welcomed the newcomers and discovered that they were French. That evening we attended a camp fire which the French scouts had organised and made our contribution to the evening. The next couple of days went like wildfire and it was soon time to say goodbye to Wiltz and make for our next port of call, Liege.

Boys and girls were scouts in Liege to the amazement of our lads, (such a phenomena was still a long way off in the U.K.) They turned up to show us the sights and swap badges. One of the highlights of the week was a trip to a glass factory, van St. Lambert. It was organised by our hosts who also provided us with an interpreter so that we could talk to the factory manager. We also held joint hikes with Belgian, French and German scouts in the local forest which was 15 miles square. We had camp fires, wide games and went swimming. Proficiency badges were gained in skills such as tracking, master cook, hiking and quartermaster.

The main highlights of the camp were the international night, the Wingate crew winning the camp sports, the weather, the welcome we received from the other scouts and the scenery. The downside included continental breakfasts, blisters, expensive food and joint male and female public toilets where most attendants were women.

The kindness towards us from the scouting brotherhood needs further mention as, at times, we were completely overwhelmed by their kindness towards us. At Ghent, the troop we stayed with were the Saint-Leven, 8th Ghent West who provided us with meals and accommodation without any charge. What was interesting about this particular troop was that it was the second oldest in Belgium having been formed in 1913. While the welcome from other scouts was special, the response we got from people in the street was amazing. When they saw you in uniform, they would come and have a chat. I met a man in Ghent when I was looking in a shop window. He saw from my scout badge that I came from Leicester and he had lived there during the war and wanted to know what things were like in post war Leicester. Scouts in uniform were charged half fare on public transport in both Belgium and Luxembourg.

We finished the trip with a day in Brussels followed by a café meal before we set off for Ostend and home. The total cost of the trip was £15 of which the greatest item was the rail fare - £8.

The group finished the year off with our annual Boxing day hike. We caught the bus from Leicester to Fleckney where we started walking to Saddington. We stopped at Debale for our lunch of turkey sandwiches and Christmas cake washed down with scalding hot tea. We then went on to Foxton Locks having been hurried on our way by a vicious snarling and snapping dog that harassed us along the path until it got the message. We spent some time at the locks watching the narrow boats making their way through them. The locks are situated on the Grand Union canal which connects with the Grand Junction Canal via the River Trent to Loughborough, Leicester and Market Harborough.

We then headed towards Gartree Prison (maximum security) which houses some of the country's dangerous criminals and terrorists. Some of the senior scouts seemed keen to get inside or perhaps they wanted to watch the football match that was going on at the time. We skirted the prison and took the path round some ploughed fields to Market Harborough until we reached the top of the road where Q lived. What a pity there was no time for tea and cakes because his mother was a superb cook and we had often sampled her cooking when we called on him. Reluctantly we boarded the bus to return to Leicester having had a gentle hike of some 11 miles and enjoyed good food, good weather and good company on the way.

In 1968 I went to St David's college at Carrog, Merionethshire in North Wales for two years with a view to taking O levels in English language and literature, Welsh history and sociology. The College was run by a Catholic order called the Divine Word Missionaries. The idea of going to St David's was to improve my education which was woefully lacking having left school at 15 with just a piece of paper to say that I had legally left school. It was my intention at that time to go to a seminary in Ireland and train for the priesthood.

My scouting activities were limited over this period although I did maintain contact through correspondence. I was unable to join the summer camp at Heythrop, the Jesuit College in Oxfordshire. It was the first camp that I had missed in 12 years.

1967 Wiltz-Luxemberg
Q Skip Mark Pratt

Adam G and Phillip Dainty on the river Witham

My wife (Mary) and daughter (Edel) 1977

Jimmy in his Bivuack at Summer Camp 1981 at Wells-Next-the-Sea

Indian Guides at Poacher Camp 1996

Summer Camp Eton Vale, Norfolk 1986
Richard Grant ASL on extreme right

Our cubs visiting at Poacher '87 for the day

Lincoln Scout Band Lead the 2000 St Georges Day Parade

Skip (Everitt) & Arkela (Brown) in the foreground 1968

During my time in Merionethshire, I joined the local Red Cross Detachment run by a Mrs Hinley, an English lady who was the life and soul of the area. Over the next couple of years I took part in fund raising events such as carol singing and helped to run fetes, organised outings for senior citizens and worked with handicapped children. Undoubtedly the highlight of my time with the Red Cross was being selected in 1969 to represent the County at the investiture of Prince Charles at Caernarvon Castle along with another student and a lecturer at the College, Father Fox. The three of us were representing a Welsh speaking county and the lecturer was American, the other student was from Northern Ireland and I was half Irish and half English.

When the great day came, I was stationed outside the castle between two Welsh Guards. I was on the route that the Royal party would take and I was ready to spring into action if any First Aid was needed. Fortunately it wasn't. I was able to observe the spectacle unhindered. Afterwards we went to the presbytery of the local Parish Priest where we met the Bishop of Mineva. His diocese covered most of Wales but not Cardiff. The Bishop was Langton Fox and he had the distinction of being the first Catholic bishop to attend a royal investiture since the reformation at which he had read the Lord's prayer in Welsh. Never mind the Royal occasion. This was some gathering in the priest's house. When we returned to the college, we had a few tales to tell the rest of the students about what was a truly memorable day.

I might not have had much to do with scouting during 1968/9 but my scouting skills were put to good use, canoeing on the River Dee which flowed by the college and had a very swift current that tested my abilities to the full. On one occasion the canoe tipped over and I was hanging upside down with my head in the water and unable to get out because the canoe was such a tight fit. I struggled and got out in the end but it was a close thing. The first aid skills I had learned in the scouts stood me in good stead with my Red Cross activities and we did plenty of hiking along the hills and dales of the Dee valley.

I moved to Donamon Castle in County Roscommen, the oldest inhabited castle in Ireland in 1970 to study philosophy and was there until 1972. I did join the scouts for the summer camp in 1972 at Carrog in the grounds of my old college, St David's in North Wales. I managed to get the rector to allow them to camp in the grounds at a very reasonable cost. We spent most of our time hiking, fishing, canoeing and sight seeing.

A party of Girl Guides had been on the site before we arrived and they warned us that they had had several tents damaged by some unruly youngsters who were camping nearby. The youngsters were from a camp run by the Social Service volunteers who were bringing deprived children from Inner City Liverpool in an old double decker bus for holidays during the summer a week at a time. The children ranged in age from 6 to 15. For most of them it was the first time they had ever had a holiday in the country or, indeed, any sort of holiday. We made ourselves known to the organisers and had one or two activities together including a memorable football match when some of their players, including their main centre forward who happened to be a girl, almost kicked our scouts off the field with their rough play. Some of their language was a bit colourful too. The captain was a 13-year-old called Brenda and our lads tackled her in a very gentle manner. She went in hard for the tackles and bowled over our lads. In the mist of time, I cannot for the life of me remember the score or who won but I do remember that the boys had a few cuts and bruises.

We had a supper and camp fire one evening. Half way through the proceedings, I was aware that we had several new faces round the fire and they were joining in the singing. Initially the children came out of curiosity but they clearly enjoyed themselves because a couple of nights later when we had a camp fire, we had several more children join us. Afterwards our 'guests' told us that they thought scouts were soppy and stuck up but having spent a week watching us, they changed their minds and, when it was time to go home, a lot of them didn't want to go back to Liverpool. Even the demon football player shed a few tears. Clearly the children had learned how to enjoy themselves without getting into trouble, probably for the first time in their lives. Some of these deprived children might have been persuaded to join the scouts when they got home. Who knows?

This was the last year that the scouts travelled to camp by lorry.

In 1970, a scout called David Woods joined the troop. He was described as being quadriplegic spastic with speech problems. He was an inspiration to us all with his determination and courage despite being confined to a wheel chair. He joined in games and activities as far as he was able. He even used to go camping. He was a very good chess player and took great delight in beating us all. He undertook a sponsored walk with his patrol taking it in turns to push him round the course.

David's mother, Mrs Eileen Woods started the spastics Society and, at this time, was vice president. She told reporters that, "The scouts have practically adopted David and he gets a tremendous amount of enjoyment from it."

Later that year, one of the scouts, John Ruddy, presented Lady Barnett, who was then President of the Leicester Spastics Society with a cheque for £93.12/6.

I left College at the end of 1972. I had decided to follow a career in the law and order field rather than progress towards the priesthood. I returned to full time scouting and took over as Scout Leader when Digger Spider Aston moved to Middleton near Manchester.

Our total income in 1973 was £413.57 which was raised by rummage sales and paper collections and a sponsored walk that raised over a £100. Our total outgoings for canoe parts, tent pegs, training manuals, compasses and cooking equipment came to £413. How's that for budgeting?

Pilgrimage – Walsingham

We took part in the Scout and Guide celebration at Walsingham in Norfolk in June. It is England's major Marian shrine. The pilgrimage was attended by scouts and guides from all over the Midlands and was led by our National Chaplain, Father Reynolds.

The procession started at half past two followed by Mass. We then walked the Golden Mile from the Catholic shrine into the village and finished off the day with a camp fire.

Our main camp that year was at Lulworth Cove in Dorset and the weather was beautiful. We camped on the cliff top and had a wonderful view of the sea. Another reason that I will always remember that camp is that in the second week a troop of Girl Guides camped nearby and their leader asked if some of our scouts would help. Apparently the girls were being examined for their country dancing badges and they needed male partners for it. The scouts' response was less than encouraging but after appealing to their better nature and some friendly persuasion, several of them eventually agreed to take part.

We all assembled on the well kept green outside the camp warden's bungalow. A portable record player was brought out and I went to sit down and enjoy the entertainment, ready to have a good laugh if the scouts made fools of themselves. Before I could do so, I was seized by the Guide Captain, a very portly lady, and propelled up and down the lawn while the scouts and guides stood back and clapped. A large lady she may have been but, by heck, she could move. I had no choice but to take it all in good part with the scouts trying to hide their grins as I fought to regain my breath. Generally speaking, it was a good afternoon.

An irate farmer turned up at the camp one day and said that two of our scouts had spat at him when he was driving his tractor. He was speaking in a broad Dorset accent so it was difficult to understand exactly what he was saying but it was to the effect, "Oi were sitting on this 'ere tractor when someone spat an' it went reit down my neck it did, reit down."

He picked out the two culprits and I was surprised. They were two of our youngest scouts and they certainly weren't the types to spit at anyone. On questioning them, it turned out that they had been standing on the old railway bridge having a competition to see who could spit the furthest and, unfortunately, the farmer had driven his tractor under the bridge at the wrong moment and had received the full torrent. Needless to say, the boys were disciplined and sent off but we did see the funny side to it.

Ferrying equipment from the lorry to the camp site

Kinver near Stourbridge was the site of our next camp and it was memorable because our young curate, Father Dolan, came with us. To have a chaplain actually camping with us was a luxury as we could have Mass on site. Normally we would hike to the nearest Church on a Sunday and it often was a hike. Father Dolan had a great sense of humour. He had an Irish name and when the Nuns, for whom he provided pastoral care, asked him which part of Ireland he came from, he took great delight in telling them, "Nottingham, Sister."

He would go hiking with the scouts but always attached himself to the group that was walking the shortest distance. On one occasion, the group that he joined had expressed their plan of completing a leisurely four to five mile walk. They finished up with a ten mile hike. It was a very tired but happy priest that arrived back at the camp that evening. What the patrol had lacked in mapping and compass skills they had made up for with comradeship and high spirits.

We had a tradition in the 64/74th that different leaders would take it in turns to go off for a drink in the evening when we were camping. There was generally a pub in the area and very often a piano near the bar round which we would gather. The locals, seeing us in scout uniforms, would generally ask us to sing and we didn't need a second invitation. We would start off with our traditional songs like Molly Malone, Ken John Peel or Riding along on the Crest of a Wave and it was never long before everyone was joining in and the noise would be loud enough to shake the rafters. There was never any drunkenness or vandalism that is connected with so many pubs today.

We didn't know what Father Dolan would think about going out for a drink and it was left to me to ask him. I needn't have worried. He said that he would love to come for drink with us. There was only one problem – if he had one, he would need to have two or even three.

Later on, the troop took part in Tramp 74, a sponsored walk round Bradgate Park in Newtown Linford. It was the home of Lady Jane Grey and parts of her house are still standing in the most beautiful setting, bracken covered hills where a herd of fallow deer roam. Several hundred pounds was collected that day and the 74th collected £92 of it.

In September, the Leicestershire scouts welcomed the chief scout, Sir Erskine William Gladstone to Quenby Hally. Quenby was once a thriving village but now, it is deserted except for the hall. It was built in 1615 and is the home of Squire de Lisle who gave permission for the rally to be held there. The proceedings started with a welcome from the County Commissioner, Lord Crawshaw followed by different district displays and presentations which included modern scouting water activities, badge training, pioneering and a mediaeval fair.

1975 kicked off with our East Division Handicraft Exhibition in which 16 of our scouts took part entering exhibits in sketches, working models, metalwork, woodwork and plaster work in the two age groups, 11-13 and 14-16. We had several individual winners but did not win the outright competition. It was surprising how many talents existed in the area.

We held a 'bring a friend' evening in an effort to increase our numbers. We held a typical scout evening. We had static displays and had a cooking demonstration on calor gas. Nine visitors came to the evening from which we gained five recruits.

Another good evening was the 'Tramps supper.' Both leaders and scouts dressed up (or down) in their ragged clothes and the most authentic dress received a prize awarded by Father Dolan. The evening was not just about dress, the scouts were urged to find out more about tramp behaviour and customs. My dress was modelled on a local tramp we all knew as 'Rum weather.' He was called that because every time I met him, he would say, "It's rum weather today, John." He called everybody John. He would never beg or ask you for money but, if you offered it, he would be grateful and shake your hand violently before continuing on his way. As far as I am aware, he never spent the money on alcohol.

Some of the tramp activities we looked at were the signs they used to mark on walls or pathways to let each other know what kind of reception they would receive from the nearby house.

The troop had concocted a menu which included old boots soup, nettle tea, fried bread and jam sandwiches, hot dogs and rough lemonade. Each team had to make a bed for the night from old newspapers and also compose a tramp song.

I set out from home having already donned my tramp costume. I was pushing an old pram that was full of bric-a-brac and rags. I certainly got a few odd looks from passers by. I made sure I was scratching when I saw them looking at me. They soon crossed over to the other side of the road and walked away.

A world Jamboree takes place every four years and, in 1975, it was being held in Norway. Leicestershire was allocated places for two leaders and 18 scouts and venture scouts to form a troop strength of four leaders and 36 scouts with Nottinghamshire. Following a short selection process the 4th had a scout, John Zemelis who was half Irish and half Ukrainian, picked to form part of the contingent. The qualifications were that you had to be between the ages of 14 and 18, you had to demonstrate that you possessed a range of scouting skills and be a good ambassador for your country and scouting. The cost of attending the jamboree was £140. Every scout was expected to have two uniforms, standardised equipment including rucksacks, adventure clothing, hiking boots, pullovers and jackets.

John was expected to raise half the amount himself and the remainder was to be raised by the troop by way of rummage sales, cheese and wine evenings, etc. The actual jamboree lasted a week. Then the scouts had a further week staying with the family of a Norwegian scout. The theme of the camp was sharing, food, fun, and fellowship. I am sure that the experience of the jamboree stayed with John for a long time.

Bronham near Bedford was the site of our summer camp, a delightful site comprising of ten acres of grassland and eight acres of woodland and there were good amenities on the site.

We held a treasure hunt in September with clues round a large area of Highfields. I played the part of a Sikh complete with turban, my face darkened and my arm in a sling. I stood outside the cinema in an area which was manly Moslem, Hindu and Sikh. The scouts had to approach me with the correct challenge, "Does it hurt mate?" to which I would reply, "Not half mate," and give them the next clue. I certainly got some strange looks from the locals before my stint was over.

The troop took part in a backwoods cooking competition. Each patrol had to gather all the wood they needed and lay and light a fire using two matches. On the menu was fish which had to be cooked on a reflector board. Fish cooked in this way was pegged on to a wooden board and stood at an angle to reflect the fire's heat. There was also pigeon which was wrapped with mud and leaves and cooked in the ashes of the fire. Carrots, potatoes, swede and onions were sliced, wrapped in tin foil and cooked in the fire. Drop scones were cooked by placing the dough on hot stones or bricks. Twists were prepared by wrapping dough round a stick and holding it over the ashes. Hot drinks were made by boiling water in a paper bag. We didn't win the competition but we had a lot of fun and plenty of interesting things to eat.

Our summer camp was a bit different that year because we joined forces with our adjacent troop and friendly rivals, the 34th St. Saviours (a Church of England sponsored group). We went to Hathersage in Derbyshire. The highlight of the camp included sheep dog trials and a trip to Sheffield. Both troops had a good time and friendships were formed that have lasted a lifetime.

The year ended with a senior citizens party. 30 old age pensioners were entertained by the cubs, scouts, venture scouts, guides and brownies. They had a five course meal with wine if they wanted it and each person received a gift before they left.

Our first full year in our new Scout Headquarters was in 1977. Financially we had just managed to keep abreast of expenditure. The heating and lighting was a large part of our costs. Our parents and supporters association continued to raise funds which saved a lot of worry because we no longer participated in a bob a job week. There had been too much abuse of the system in that the scouts were often not paid the right rate for the job. They would literally be paid a bob for what could have been a whole day's work.

A Jubilee Scout and Guide fair was held in April. One of the star attractions was the Leicester Girl Guide Band. There was a cake competition, a bottle stall, games, a white elephant stall, groceries, ice creams, comics and raffles. Admission cost 10p. There was a dance in the evening with tickets at 60p. Both events were roaring successes and brought in much needed revenue.

Rod Essex the County Commissioner for Leicestershire opening the new headquarters of the 74th in 1976 in the presence of the Parish Priest Rev Dean Murdock and the Guide Commissioner

St. Hughes College in Tollerton in Nottinghamshire was our venue for the summer camp that year. We had 12 scouts, 3 leaders, 2 wives and three children. The cost of the week was £14. No scout was allowed to bring more than £5 spending money that was paid into the camp bank which was administered by a leader. The idea of this was to prevent the scouts from spending all their money in one go and then being miserable for the rest of the week. I can remember one scout some years ago at his first camp. It was in the days before we ran a camp bank and this lad had spent all his money on the first day. We thought he would be miserable as a result but he said, "I haven't a penny left but I'm enjoying myself."

In November, the troop went on a visit to Loughborough National Steam Museum and travelled from Loughborough to Rothley via Woodhouse Eaves. As well as the trip on the steam train, we went round the locomotive sheds and the railway museum.

Pope John Paul's visit to Coventry 1982.
350,000 pilgrims present Catholic Scouts and guides camped over the weekend near the papal rostrum and provided a guard of honour.

This was a significant year in my Scouting career as I moved to Lincoln City in 1982 some 55 miles away in order to start a new job as a probation officer. Leaving my old troop after 27 years as both man and boy was quite a wrench. After settling in our new house, I got a touch of the scouting fever. It is hard to explain this to the uninitiated but is the result of seeing scouting as not just a past-time but as a way of life. However, my wife did not share my enthusiasm despite my best efforts to convert her. Following the urge to get involved again, I decided to contact the District Commissioner only to find it was easier said than done. There was no central headquarters and no listed numbers in the phone book. I eventually found out that there was a sports shop in Lincoln and the manager of it was an Assistant District Commissioner and, through him, I got the address of the District Commissioner, Len Foster.

He introduced me to several groups in the locality. After some deliberation, I decided to join the 28th Greenland Troop which was the nearest to my home. It was a fairly new but progressive group. I was made very welcome by the Group Scout leader, Mike Kelly and the Scout Leader Bernie and his assistant, Roy Lee. The 28th was one of the biggest groups in Lincoln but it didn't have its own headquarters. We met in the Church Centre which was run by the joint Ministry of the Church of England and the United Reform Church. The group had two scout troops, two cub packs, a venture group well as Guides and brownies. Later on, they had Rainbows and Beavers as well. In total, there was a scout membership of 150. Our two troops were called Saxons and Vikings. I joined the Saxon or, as it was called, the Friday Troop.

Imagine my surprise when I discovered that the local Scout Troop, the 28th Greenlands had a maroon and white neckerchief similar to the one I had worn in Leicester. While I was with the 28th, a competition was held asking us to design a suitable group badge that could be worn on the back of the neckerchief. Lots of designs were submitted and the one chosen was a triangular shape badge with a green background. In the top half was a Viking helmet with a wavy blue line beneath it and, at the bottom, was the Roman numeral XXVIII. The colour green was for the green fields, the area where we lived. The helmet was for the national walk, the Viking Way which runs for some 147 miles from Humberside to Rutland and is situated at the back of our estate. The wavy blue line represents the River Witham, our local river. Finally, the Roman numerals are for the 28th, our group number.

The 28th was an open sponsored troop which meant that the scouts were of all denominations or none at all. I was kept on my toes because I knew that if I was talking about religion, the scouts might not know what I was talking about.

This was highlighted for me when some new recruits came up from the cubs. Filling in their record cards, I asked one of the boys to which religion he belonged. He looked at me in a puzzled manner and said, "I don't know. I will have to ask my Mum and let you know."

Members of the 28th Lincoln (Greenlands) Scout Group with my daughter in 1986

Most of the leaders in Lincoln had an air-force background and lived within a few miles of Waddington air Base.

One of the first functions I attended was a leaders' camp at Sudbooke, our local camp site situated some three miles from Lincoln. This was where I was to be formally initiated into the 28th. However, I was blooded in an unexpected way. It was getting dark and I switched on the generator to provide some lighting when the handle shot off and struck me in the face. It gave me a black eye and a cut and bleeding nose. I was seeing stars for some time. Seeing the force with which the handle hit, I was lucky I wasn't more seriously hurt. Needless to say, it caused me to take a week off work.

My first scout night highlight was the troop coming up ceremony with three cubs wishing to join the scouts. The ceremony is important as it heralds the progress of the lad through the movement. The cub is not joining as an outsider but is more of a junior scout who has probably spent three years as a cub. The cubs come into the room and every one is greeted and has his hand shaken by the scout leader. The troop then come to the alert and the cub leader, (Barbara McLeish) introduced the cubs to me and gave a potted history of their progress so far. The leaders of the patrols which they were going to join, stood behind them while the cubs were formally welcomed into the troop and given their badges and patrol flashes. The cubs did not have to be invested into the movement as a new recruit would have been because they had already invested in the cub pack and were just moving on to the next stage of their scouting career.

The following week, we visited a neighbouring group, the 7th St. Faith's and had a joint programme which included cooking a meal and a survival demonstration. Later that month, we entertained the 15th Lincoln Girl Guides. We laid on refreshments and music and had a general games evening. This event was a great success and there were requests to have it repeated. I must say that the scouts had smartened themselves up when they knew the girls were going to attend.

We had several scouts entered for the Fireman's and First Aid badges. Also several cubs coming up into our group in June and that boosted our numbers up to36.

Most of this month's programme was taken up with pre-camp preparations inspecting tents, overhauling and demonstrating the correct use of stoves – maths and paraffin, both single and double burners. July saw the holding of the troop meeting in Sudbrooke Park and splitting into three work teams in order to help complete a camp fire circle gate and arrange an entrance. Refreshments were provided. At the end of the night, five scouts were invested under the trees with the birds singing in the background. It was a beautiful setting and the sense of occasion uplifted everyone.

The under 13 team came third in the annual sports day. Overall the 28th came fourth. We had a night hike to Sudbrooke in July with each patrol travelling a different route. Each hike was eight miles and the scouts were taken to the starting points by private transport. Each scout took a packed 'lunch' and something for breakfast. A leader accompanied each patrol but they were only there to observe and they would only intervene in an absolute emergency.

The hike kicked off at 8p.m. and the estimated time of arrival was 11 o'clock. Everyone arrived safely although the last patrol did not arrive until midnight having gone astray with their map reading. There were lots of stories exchanged about their adventures over supper and the things they had done and seen on the way. One patrol said that they had been approached by a farmer with a shot gun who thought they were poachers looking for game. After supper, there were lots of tired legs and they belonged to the leaders. Everyone turned in exhausted but feeling they had achieved something even if it was only the younger ones conquering their fear of the dark or the older ones honing their leadership skills and gaining confidence in their ability to lead and make decisions. After breakfast – eggs, bacon, sausage, beans, bread, butter, jam and gallons of tea, the troop was conveyed back to H.Q. We knew the hike had been a success when they all asked, "Can we do it again?"

We did have another night hike in September with our other troop, Viking, but this time we used C.B. sets to keep in touch.

The scouts obtained a number of proficiency badges through the year including Fireman, First Aid, Camper, hiker and Mechanic. A number of Scout standard and advanced Scout standard awards were made.

Fund raising activities continued. Over 70 adults attended our district social which the troop organised. There were refreshments and a buffet. The event made £100. We had a tramps supper in November with invited and uninvited guests. The tramps formed into four groups and called themselves Billy's Boys, Lenny's Lads, Jeff's Gents and John's Layabouts. We had games such as musical newspapers, tramp objects and rubbish bin carrying.

We rounded off the year with two events, a display of fencing by the Venture scouts and a treasure hunt, 'Operation Goodwill,' a district event which was a treasure hunt round Lincoln. The entry fee was at least two tins of food which was then donated to local charities. The patrol donating the most tins was given a prize. One patrol brought 150 tins.

We started off 1984 with a social event at R.A.F. Swinderby. 16 leaders from the 28th troop went with their wives and/or girl friends.

In February we commenced training for the Master-at-Arms badge. To obtain this, the scout had to be proficient in one of the following;- boxing, judo, wrestling, karate or ju-jitsu. Over a three month period, the scouts had to demonstrate forward and backward rolls, break falls and demonstrate methods of defence and attack against assault by fist, foot, club and knife. Six scouts gained their badges.

Bernie, the Scout leader left and handed over a thriving troop. Ray Lee became Skip. We also had a new Assistant leader, Martin who immediately became known as Chip.

A group camp was held at Walesby in June. It is an H.Q. camp site covering acres of woodland and fields and provides a hundred different camp sites.

An Incident hike was held in July. Various scenes were presented at different points on the walk such as someone suffering an epileptic fit or a heart attack or they would find a lost tourist or come on a scene of a car crash. One of these must have been so realistic that a member of the public reported it to the police and we had a police car complete with siren come to investigate. In all of these situations, the scouts were marked on their knowledge, actions, leadership qualities and organisation.

A father and son camp was held in October at Sudbrooke Park but, at the first sign of rain, all the fathers bar one, Mr Doncaster, went home much to the disgust of their sons.

Other events included orienteering and a musical evening and I took part in the Annual Poacher Hike – never again. It was a 38 mile hike across the Lincolnshire Wolds. There were members from many organisations taking part, youth clubs, Red Cross, Combined Forces etc. Hikers were in teams of four. Prizes were awarded for the fastest team and the fastest individual. Everyone who completed the course got a certificate. We started at Linwood. Everyone signed in and their kit was checked and weighed. It had to include a first aid kit. The teams had to go through check points at intervals on the course. Cold drinks were provided along the way and as it grew colder, these were replaced with hot soup and pasties.

Our team included Ray Lee, our Scout leader, an Assistant leader, Chip, a Venture scout and yours truly. At 41 I was the oldest to take part and the Venture scout, at 17, was the youngest. We went well for the first fourteen miles. Then Chip dropped out with blisters and, at the 19mile stage, the Venture scout called it a day. He was suffering from cramp. We valiant two carried out until Skip Lee retired with a sprained ankle. I was very much on my own but I picked up a few strays from other teams on the way. There were about a dozen of us and not one of us was with anyone from the team that we had started with. One or two had to be helped to the next check point. Several gave up with minor medical problems such as exhaustion, blisters or sprains. I leaned against a tree and snatched a bite to eat and then ploughed on with five others.

By the time I reached the finish, I was tired but exhilarated by the fact that the 'old one' had finished the course when the youngsters had dropped out. My time was 18 hours and 4 minutes (2.2 miles an hour). We had been slowed down because we had had to help others but it was the fact of being one of those finishing when over 200 of the others had dropped out. 300 had started.

Now for something completely different. In February 1985, I became a fashion model. The 28th had organised a fashion show in conjunction with C & A fashions and we had to provide the models. These were leaders, guides, scouts, brownies, cubs and parents. A catwalk was erected in the scout room and we strutted along it, posed and did our stuff. The entry fee was 50p and some of the clothes were raffled.

We had a night time wide game in Hartsholme Country Park. The scouts were divided into groups and the object of the game was to locate the other team's flag while defending their own. Each scout had a piece of cotton wool attached to his arm and if that was snatched, he had to return to a centre point and was out of the game for a while until a new life was obtained. The winner of the game was the team that had seized the most flags.

One group had caught sight of movement behind a bush and, keeping quiet, they had crept up on it. They were just about to pounce when they realised it was a courting couple, not their opponents at all. The couple had chosen the wrong spot at the wrong time. History has not recorded what was actually said between the two parties.

My first summer camp with the 28th was at Irthlingborough in Northamptonshire. There were 12 scouts, my wife, daughter and her friend, Jillian Hillis. We had a fabulous week visiting Rockingham Castle, canoeing, going on a canal boat trip as well as the usual scout activities. My daughter tried her hand at canoeing. She stepped into the canoe which she thought was secured but it wasn't and it turned over throwing her into the water. Fortunately the only thing that was hurt was her pride but she was more careful the next time. The main highlight was the friendships that we experienced with some Red Cross volunteers and cadets who were camping near us and looking after several children. We had several activities together including camp fires and a trip on the canal. The boys became very fond of the children and the feeling was reciprocated but the week went far too quickly. We went our separate ways with many happy memories.

We held a car wash in October which raised £70 for the troop funds. We also attended a District Activity day which had a

Mediaeval theme. Activities included archery, sedan chair racing, slippery pole and stocks.

10 August 1985 Irthlingborough in Northamptonshire
Chip ASL standing at the back and the author in front
with a red cross hat on

On the 10th of November, the 28th hosted the Chief Scout Award presentations at which the County Commissioner, Dr Edwin Gobbett awarded certificates and badges to 13 scouts from our district. We were thanked for our hospitality but particularly for our tea and excellent buns.

Unfortunately Skip Lee resigned as Scout leader owing to business commitments although he stayed on as a part time instructor.

1986 started with a competition night in which the patrols had to build a free standing flag pole using ropes, spars and a hoist and break and fly a flag. Stag patrol won the contest. They also built the highest flag pole, 14 feet. This was a good exercise because the flag pole is the focal point of the camp. It is where the scouts fall in for prayers, notices and presentations each day and it is the scouts' job to build the flag pole. The duty patrol of the day has to hoist the flag each morning, lead the prayers and lower the flag in the evening. Knowledge of flags is also required so that the scouts know which flag takes preference over another if there are several flags flying and, with the Union Jack, it is important to know that it is flown the right way up. If it is upside down, it means distress and if it is flown at half mast, it means that someone has died.

My daughter Edel lined up with the Buffalo Patrol for Inspection

There was a flurry of activity in January and February with a District cross country and wide game on the West Common and a return visit to the 9th Lincoln troop. We attended a meeting about living off the land in February which included which plants were edible and which were poisonous and how to filter muddy water.

This was followed at a later date by a practical excursion and demonstration out in the wild.

The 28th competed again in the swimming gala in March. We supported our swimmers with great enthusiasm but achieved little success in the event. We held a computer evening later in the month and several scouts began their training for the computer badge. We held a training camp for patrol leaders and assistant patrol leaders at Walesby Forest in May.

Our summer camp was held in Eaton vale near Norwich. The patrol leaders held training sessions for their patrols on how to pack a rucksack, tent pitching, kit layout, knots and lashing. Just before we left for camp, we had to say goodbye to Chip who was leaving us for work purposes. We were sure to miss his cheerful face but to make sure that we didn't forget him we had a shield made with his name on it which was to be presented for the 'Best scout of the month' award. We were lucky to obtain the services of another Assistant Scout Leader, Richard Grant, a biologist who now lives in Australia.

Supper time at Summer camp 1986

The week before we left for camp, our Thursday group – Viking – went to Great Tower, an HQ campsite near Windermere. Their activities included climbing Helvellyn (2,700 feet), swimming in Lake Windermere, a trip to Holker Hall and joining a communal camp fire with Dutch and Belgian scouts. The best scout of the camp was Andrew Preston. (He's now a probation officer at Boston.) The most promising scout was Richard Wilson and the 'Wally' of the week award was gained by James Preston, Andrew's brother who wore the badge with pride. The scouts ended the camp with a presentation for the leaders, Skip and Mrs Doc, for making the camp such an enjoyable event.

My nephew, Kevin Costello, joined the 74th Sacred Heart Leicester troop following my move to Lincoln. He gained his Chief Scouts Award but sadly left the movement at 15 years.

We rounded off the year with a Christmas party and disco and invited the guides. The evening got off to a slow start on account of the shyness of some of the scouts mixing with the girls, however, when the scouts realised the girls were human and didn't bite, the evening went with a swing.

1987 was another busy year. We issued a Uni hoc challenge to the district, played chess at Saxilby HQ, had a patrol leaders night out (ten pin bowling), had a disco, attended the patrol leaders training course at Sudbrooke and hosted the District handicraft competition. I had another duty to perform as a judge at the District Camping Competition at Shackwell Hollow, the Stamford and Bourne District site. There were ten patrols taking part who had all won through from their districts in order to compete in the final. Eight scouters judged the competition and we were all experienced campers and leaders.

In May we had a treasure hunt, a survival weekend and an incident hike. We had a police and bike night in July when a local officer spoke to the scouts about being bike wise and taking steps to security mark their cycles. He also gave them some tips re safeguarding their machines from being stolen or, at least, make it harder for the thieves to take it.

The Poacher 87 International Mini Jamboree was held at the Lincolnshire show ground. The theme was ancient tribes and the camp was split into six sections, the Corieani, Angles, Saxons, Viking, Normans and Romans. Our camp was the Saxons and our two groups combined. We had 22 scouts, 4 leaders, my wife and daughter and six helpers. We called our patrols Broadsword, Celts, Longbows and Saxons. Also in our sub group were guides from Windsor, Scunthorpe, Lincolnshire and Humberside and scouts from South Yorkshire, Cleethorpes and Lincoln. We also had scouts and guides from Scandinavia, Singapore and New Zealand.

Our cubs visiting for the day at Poacher 1987

We were kept busy with adventurous activities on and off the camp site as well as creative past times. Games included six a side football, Volley ball, Super stars and sedan chair racing. There were service projects throughout the week with scouts and guides going into the community to lend a hand and welcome some of the less fortunate members of the community, Hospital patients, the handicapped and senior citizens.

28th Cooks at Poacher 2000

The emphasis at Poacher camp is on fun, adventure and mixing, not that these aren't in every camp but a greater influence is put on the youngsters being free while the leaders and helpers do the spade work, cooking and administration, things that would normally have been done by the scouts. Great store was put on the young people having a good time but this did not mean the leaders were left out. We wandered round the site to see what was going on or took the opportunity for some quiet relaxation in the leaders' club in easy chairs and have a foot massage while listening to relaxing music. The only time we saw the scouts was at breakfast before they started their activities, at lunch when they dropped in for a sandwich before heading off again and at dinner when the day's activities ended. We would find out what they were up to over meals, what new skills they had acquired and which new friendships they had formed.

The evening's events started at half past seven with concerts performed by groups in their national costumes, discos, campfires and dances, the whole scene being lit up by laser lights.

One of our patrol leaders, Peter Moore, broke his arm on the second day. I took him to the hospital and informed his step-father (Patrick Sweeny, one of my ex scouts) who met us when we returned to camp several hours later with Peter's arm in a plaster cast. His step-father wanted to take him home. "No way," said Peter, "I'm enjoying camp and I intend to get my money's worth, so I'm staying." And he stayed.

Poacher 1987 at Lincolnshire Show Ground
Mary, Ally and Edel at the front

One of our patrol leaders, Mark Whyatt, was interviewed by a reporter form the Lincolnshire Echo. When he asked what the highlight of the camp was, he said, "Meeting other Scouts and Guides from all over the world." He also said that he had had a 'stab' at fencing and was looking forward to trying his hand at other activities during the week.

There was some wet and windy weather but the elements could not dampen the spirits of the campers. The Lord Lieutenant of Lincolnshire, Sir Henry Neville, visited the camp as did the Chief Scout, Michael Walsh. The County Scout and Guide Commissioners also attended.

It was my idea of heaven seeing the 3,000 young and not so young enjoying themselves for a week in each other's company.

The mini city had its own security service, banking facilities, shops, fire service, hospital, press and worship tent. A camp Newspaper called the Poacher Link was printed each day and was produced by the Link International Fellowship. It contained an exchange and mart section as well as witty anecdotes such as;

Pat Cliffe – I married Peter because I thought he was rich

Peter Cliffe – I married Pat because I thought she was rich

And they both lived in poverty

The moral of this story is – always check his bank statement, girls.

The camp fire is one of the great traditions of the scout movement and it captured my imagination from the word go. Sitting round a blazing log fire with the smoke curling up into a starry night and the heat of the fire giving a warm glow and being surrounded by scouts wrapped in their camp fire blankets and every one singing their hearts out.

Once everything had been organised, every patrol was asked to contribute an item whether it be a song, a yell or a sketch. Then the scout leader and his assistants would put the show together and time it. My old Skipper used to say, "A good camp fire has a beginning, a middle and an end." It sounds obvious but it needs thinking about.

To get things going, the leader starts with a rousing greeting. My own favourite was, "Every one join us in this wonderful occasion and with every hand above the flames lifted, we shall with magic touch be enlifted."

Author's camp fire blanket

Favourite rousing songs were One man went to Mow, Green grow the Rushes O, and Ten Green Bottles. As the camp fire progressed the voices would build up into a crescendo with yells like, "boomalacka, boomalacka," and "We're from Lincoln, Mighty, Mighty Lincoln." This was followed by action songs and everybody participated with – We are Red man, Old and Quaint and The Grand old Duke of York. The latter part of the camp fire included quieter songs – In Dublin's Fair City, Clementine and Poor Old Joe. Finally there would be a hymn – Kum by yah (Come by here Lord) or the Scout hymn. Prayers followed. A couple of my favourites were Taps and As the Camp Fire Fades.

An important part of a camp fire is etiquette. The leader needs to have control of what is going on. Encourage enthusiasm and make sure that the participants enjoy themselves but, at the same time, be strict with disruptive behaviour. The golden rule was that every individual effort was applauded no matter how good or bad the item was. What was important was the effort that had been put into it. If the participant was poor, then a little bit of encouragement would not go amiss. Ridicule or rejection would deter them from trying again. Etiquette also demanded that everyone kept quiet while other presenters were doing their bit. In other words, they were expected to show consideration to others. A camp fire must not be too long or people will start to get bored. A good leader will delegate but still keep control so that people do not get fed up with his voice.

There was a danger at one time that camp fires would be abolished in favour of mobile phones, the internet and other innovations. It was felt that the tradition would die out but there was a revival in the 1990s.

Long may the camp fire tradition continue.

My ideal way to depart this life if I was given the choice would be sitting round a blazing log fire with family and friends and feeling close to nature, having a nice glass of wine or cup of tea and singing my heart out as the flames leap up to infinity.

The 1988 summer camp was held at Birch Hall in Yorkshire. The site was a grass fields bounded on three sides by a stream and with easy access to the Yorkshire Moors. Activities reflected the outdoor life, canoeing, pony trekking, swimming, hiking and travelling on a steam train right across the moors. It was meant to be a two day one night expedition. We had gone over the route with the scouts. Their clothing and equipment had been checked and emergency procedures discussed. The scouts had to report in to check points along the route to make sure that they were going in the right direction. Things seemed to be going well on the first day right up to mid-afternoon but the trio failed to report at a couple of check points after that and, as time got on, concern set in. In the meantime, the bulk of the scouts had gone swimming. I was the only leader in camp and I had my daughter Edel with me and my niece Paula as well as two sick scouts. At about 6pm, the Group Scout leader and Camp leader, Malcolm Moore, rushed into camp and explained that he and another leader were going to look for the missing scouts. He also informed me that the transport bringing the other scouts back from swimming had suffered a shattered windscreen and could not be driven. Could I take the one remaining vehicle and rescue the stranded party.

That left me with a problem. What was I going to do with two sick scouts and the girls? There wouldn't be enough room to take them in the van as well as the scouts I had to bring back. Then I had a brainwave. Camping nearby was a contingent of Army Cadets from Lincolnshire. I approached the major in charge and asked if I could leave my four charges in his care and collect them later. Not only did he offer to help but said that the cadets could assist in searching for the missing scouts. Not wanting to make things more dramatic than they really were, I told him that things weren't at crisis point yet. The cadets were apparently taking part in summer manoeuvres with four hundred other cadets from all over the country.

By the time I reached the stranded swimmers and returned to the camp, nightfall was approaching. I went across to collect my four charges. The major told me that they had been put in the care of the female NCOs. They had been given a meal and bedded down for the night. He suggested that I left them there and collected them in the morning to which I readily agreed.

I went over to collect my charges the first thing next morning. The foursome were sitting up in bed and being served breakfast by the NCOs. I was asked if I would like breakfast but I quickly declined. I had seen the porridge and the scrambled eggs being served up in solid wedges. The only difference between the two was that the porridge was whiter. The four of them had had a great time. Before she left, Edel persuaded one of the NCOs to write a note saying that she had spent the night with 60 rifles, 6 machine guns, 2 heavy machine guns and hundreds of rounds of ammunition.

When we got back to the camp, we were told that the missing scouts had been found. They had deviated from their route and, with night approaching, had set up camp for the night and, after breakfast, they had got back on to the correct route. It had been a hectic day and a half. One of the heartening things of the episode was the cooperation and willingness to help that we received from the Cadets.

We had a group outing to RAF Finningly in September followed by a hike to Lady Bower Reservoir and Dovedale in Derbyshire.

Our main activity in October was a night hike to Laughterton, Gainsborough District site. In the run up to Christmas we had a Scout Fayre and a Snobs' dinner in December with candles, champagne and canapés. Another highlight that month was one of our scouts, Peter Moore, being presented with his Chief Scouts Award by the County Commissioner. The final event of the year was the grand Christmas prize draw, the first prize being a mini stereo system. Second prize was a hamper and the third was a rack of wine. Tickets were 20p and they sold like hot cakes. All the prizes were donated so it was all revenue for the group.

1989 started on a sad note when we were told of the death of the very Reverend Canon Murdock, the parish priest of the Sacred Heart Church. He was also the sponsor of the 64/74 Leicester Scouts and had supported them over many years.

From a sad event to a happy one – David Everitt, the nephew of my old Scout leader was ordained a priest and sent to work in Livingstone in Africa. David had been a member of Fox patrol when I had been a young leader.

An article appeared in the Leicester Mercury in December 1988 telling the story of David Woods who had joined our Leicester troop in 1970. After attending Mass at the Lady of Victories in Market Harborough, he had turned to his wife, Thelma and said, "I love you." Thus ending 36 years of silence. Now Thelma was trying to raise £3,500 to buy him a foot operated computer that he would be able to use and would allow him to communicate. The machine would have 300 phrases and, when he pressed a switch with his left foot, the voice would read out one of the phrases. Until that day, David had only been able to say yes and no with difficulty. David had visited Lourdes, the Marian shrine in France, when he was in the scouts and the group had supported him on his pilgrimage. When he was with the scouts one evening, he had showed them his expertise in morse. He did this by tapping a foot to make a light bulb flash.

The scouts started collecting to raise money for David's magic computer. They raised £55 by organising a senior citizens' dinner. Without doubt, David is a remarkable young man who deserves all the help he can get to make his life more comfortable for him and his wife.

We held the Brant Road fun run in May. This event was initially run by the Church centre but was taken over by the 28th in 1997. There were two races, the punishing 6 mile run up Waddington Hill, (it certainly wasn't for the faint hearted) and a shorter one mile run on the flat for children and less energetic adults. Everyone who finished got a medal and the runners' times were recorded. Parents and leaders acted as the marshals and the guides provided the refreshments. A PA system was also employed to keep the spectators informed on what was happening. 250 runners took part, each of them paying a £3 fee which covered the cost of the medals and refreshments leaving the remainder for group funds.

We attended a Friendship 98 District Scout camp in September and invited the 9th Lincoln to spend an evening with us. We held a treasure hunt, a cycle camp and a group night hike. In November we organised a compass bearing night on South Common, had a swimming night and a First Aid incident activity.

1990 heralded in another busy year with activities such as Go-karting, archery, rafting, training camp at Walesby Forest and a casualty simulation night. Proficiency badges gained included camp cook, quartermaster and back woodsman. The highlight of the year was the Lincoln District Gang show held at the Theatre Royal in Lincoln with some 90 participants. The Lincoln District scout band also took part. The show consisted of sketches, songs and dance routines and was staged over three nights plus a Saturday matinee. In addition to the actors, there was a team working behind the stage doing wardrobe, lighting, choreography, props and make up as well as the front of house staff. These were members of the Scout Fellowship, leaders who did not have time to run a section but would turn out and help on special occasions.

The Gang of 1990 (including James Wilson, Peter and Philip Moore and Marc Whyatt from the 28th Lincoln Group

Some years previously when we were looking for a way to improve our finances, someone had suggested a paper collection and we decided that a monthly collection was worth trying. Initially the group worked in conjunction with the Council but things weren't working out too well and we switched to a private contractor. This arrangement was successful for a while but with the price of paper fluctuating to a degree we could not guarantee a regular and stable return. Consequently we set up a scheme in which parents as well as scouts, guides, brownies and beavers all participated.

Helpers went round designated routes collecting papers and magazines that householders had left out for collection which was taken to our headquarters where willing helpers loaded it. On average we collected 6-7 tons a week. Local shops were very helpful especially our neighbourhood travel agents, 'Trips Travel,' who gave us all their old brochures and the Co-op who allowed us the use of their trolleys to collect the paper. The project was so successful that we were collecting more paper in our neighbourhood than the council. When this came to the attention of City Hall, they approached us with a scheme that would guarantee that they would pay us a fixed amount every month regardless of how the price of paper was fluctuating. The price had been swinging from £40 a ton to £15. So, once more, we were reunited with the council and enjoyed a steady income of £300, not bad for three hours work a month!

We weren't only raising money to buy new equipment and tentage but we were funding various projects with our paper collection money but the monthly collection raised the public profile of the group and put us on show to the community and helped form ties that were important to both the group and local residents. Over the years that I was involved with the 28th, paper collection was probably our greatest and most regular source of income.

In 1991, guide lines were issued for girls in scouting which was built on advice given to the movement during 1990. The Saxon group received its first girl scout in 1993. If I am honest, I must admit that I was against the idea of having girls in scouting as I felt that those who wanted adventure and excitement could always join the guides. I was also visualising all the problems that could arise in mixed gender company, camping for example.

I received a terrible shock in 1991 on being told that Laurence Brown 'Q', my old scout leader and friend had died. He was a scout leader for 25 years and for ten years, he had been the District Commissioner of Leicester East District. He was a man of great organisational ability. Apart from his job as a teacher and his religion, scouting was his life. He wasn't married and threw all his spare time into scouting. Laurence had collapsed coming out of church and was admitted to Leicester General Hospital with pneumonia. He died two weeks later aged 54. His funeral was attended by several hundred scouts, leaders, parents and dignitaries from the scouting world. His coffin was draped with the union jack and the troop flag and was adorned with religious, academic and scouting mementoes. The scout song which had been written by Ralph Reader was sung at this grave side.

"Now as I start upon my chosen way, in all I do, my thoughts, my work, my play, grant as I promise to be the best, the best that I can be."

Laurence was a great loss both in terms of personal friendship which had spanned 25 years but also to scouting. His energy was boundless and his door was always open for help and advice. The Ventures even had a designated room in his house for their meetings. Rest in peace, old chum.

Venture Scouts and leaders do a dance routine for the senior citizens Christmas Dinner in 1991

Senior Citizens Party 1991 at Church Centre

Summer camp was held at Waddecar in West Lancashire. Waddecar is a country camp site set in the beautiful Forest of Bowland and covers 21 acres. It is situated on the River Brock with open access to Bleasdale Fells. The nearest town is Preston. Blackpool is 20 miles away. The site was ideal for pioneering, fishing, ornithology, nature trails and hiking. The site boasted an archery range, a climbing tower and a permanent orienteering course with instructors available to provide tuition if it was needed. The troop also organised its own activities such as trail laying, tracking, bivouacking, crazy camp sports and days out.

1992 started with a myriad of activities including a talk from the RSPCA Inspector, outdoors cooking night, joint camp fires with the

Girl Guides, quiz nights, parents' evening and the Senior Citizens Christmas party and a course at the local fire station for the Fireman's badge.

The highlight of the year was Poacher 92 which was the second Poacher camp I had attended as a leader. The theme was 'famous people from Lincolnshire' and the six sub camps were: Isaac Newton, the Pilgrim Fathers, Matthew Flinders, John Smith, Hereward the Wake and John Wesley. Our sub camp was Isaac Newton comprising of 626 scouts and guides out of a total of 4,576 at the camp. Countries that were represented there other than the UK were Uganda, Finland, Egypt, Japan, USA, Canada and New Zealand. New activities included Highland games, ugly bug ball, rodeo show, Stage Coach Rock and Roll show and Olympic games.

The 28th won the hockey final beating a team from Scunthorpe, 4-2.

The main non-scouting item at Poacher was the white helmets, the Royal Signals motor cycle display team which is the oldest and best known military display team in the world having been formed in 1927.

We were informed when we reported for the 1992 Gang show that in 1990, the show had made a profit of £1,600 which was distributed between the Council's Len Foster Expedition fund, £800, St Christopher's Special School, £300, the City toy library, £200 and £100 each to the County Hospital, the Lincolnshire Narrow Boat Trust and the Brandy Home of Rest for Horses.

Three aims had been set down with our first Gang show - to provide good family entertainment, bring all branches of scouting and guides together and raise some money for local charities. The show successfully achieved all three.

The troop received a Certificate of Merit from the Colonel Saunders Environmental Awards which was developed and sponsored by Kentucky Fried Chicken and the Tidy Britain group. We received our award for our efforts in helping to keep the local shopping centre clear of litter and conducting surveys about environmental issues amongst the local shoppers.

We included some new activities to our usual ones in 1993 such as cyclo-cross, archery sessions, a talk on Bosnia and a barbeque with the Guides. April saw the continuation of Operation Cleanup which was first launched in 1991 when the troop cleaned up the area around our headquarters. We filled up 20 large black sacks with rubbish which included broken glass, cigarette ends, beer cans, cardboard boxes and other unpleasant messes. We also got shoppers to sign a petition for more litter bins which we presented to the council. We also asked for recycling facilities in the area. This was part of the National Litter Campaign.

The Lincoln District held a recruitment drive in the Waterside shopping centre in Lincoln in June and the 28th helped man the stall. A deal of interest was shown in the various displays and numerous leaflets were handed out and many enquiries were received.

Summer camp was held at Squirrels Wood, Burghwallis, near Doncaster that year. Activities undertaken included abseiling, bivouacking, shooting, archery, crazy camp sports and a conservation 100 project. Badges were gained in camp cooking and backwoods.

The latter part of the year saw a parallel programme for older scouts, 14 – 16, which included using a climbing wall, a winter camp, ten pin bowling, casualty simulation, leadership skills and hikes. The main proficiency badge training was for the junior Airman.

The County Camping competition is an annual event in which the best patrols in each area compete for the trophies. All the participating patrols would receive a certificate and an outline of comments and, depending on the marks they had gained would receive a gold, silver or bronze tent peg. The competition started on a Saturday morning and finished on Sunday evening. The eight judges were all experienced Scout leaders and camped on the site the night before and received briefing sessions so that they were fully prepared for the next two days. The patrols were expected to be established teams, not ones that had been put together for the occasion. In case of sickness, two substitutes could be allowed but had to be a patrol leader or an assistant patrol leader. There were ten patrols taking part, consisting of at least four scouts in each patrol and they all had to be below the age of 15 on the day of the camp. They had to be fully equipped. Scouts were allowed to cook on any type of stove except for Saturday tea and Sunday lunch which had to be cooked on a wood fire. The wood for this was provided.

The competition was judged on the patrol's ability to run their own camp. They had to choose their own menus and were judged for their variety, content and their skill and organisation needed to cook the food. Between meals, the scouts were expected to organise their own daily programme. The judges had to receive a copy of their plans for this as well as their menus and the costing, names and addresses of each member of the patrol and phone numbers of parents and leaders. A high standard was expected in camping skills, punctuality, hygiene, presentation and preparation of meals, consideration for each other and working as a patrol.

The entry fee was £8 for each patrol and it was hoped that each district would assist the patrols by paying their camping fee and transportation costs. After the event, marking sheets would be sent to the troop leaders and the District Commissioner. If a particular patrol had not performed well, they would be given advice on where they went wrong and what they could do to improve. The whole idea was not to create 'super-dooper' patrols but rather to enable the scouts to gain additional experience.

An incident that sticks in my mind during one of these competitions was, on inspecting one patrol's kitchen after the scouts had had their evening meal and washed up, everything was found to be immaculate, in fact the frying pan looked as if it was brand new. I was suspicious and had a poke around and eventually found a set of dirty billy cans hidden in some undergrowth at the back of their kitchen. On calling up the patrol leader and asking for an explanation, he said that they always carried a special set which they kept purely for competitions.

Needless to say, they did not win and the scouts were left in no doubt about our displeasure.

I was one of the judges of this competition for seven years and, though it was hard work, it was a thoroughly good experience. Most of the judges slept under canvas and our meals were provided for us as the judging took all our time. We were constantly on the go. The 28th never actually won but one year they came a creditable 4th.

In 1994, the Lincoln Greenland troop was the largest in Lincoln District with over 150 members. We required a constant supply of assistant leaders to join the 22 we already had.

28th Lincoln (Saxon) Troop in 1994
Leaders Bosun S/L, Stuart Brown A/SL

This year saw the first issue of our new group magazine called Greenland Gossiper. That is exactly what we wanted it to be. We included planned events, our involvement in the Gang Show, monies raised, progress made by individual scouts as well as news about individual scouts and leaders.

In November, we had a group bonfire at Waddington Nurseries, each section contributing towards the cost of the fireworks.

It was heartening to hear that our group Scout Leader, Kim was making steady progress following serious injuries caused when he was knocked down by a car during the course of his work as a traffic warden. Besides other injuries, he had suffered loss of speech and memory.

I attended the 74th Leicester Scouts Jubilee Mass, giving thanks for fifty years of scouting in Sacred Heart Parish. The lectern had been made by scouts with the guidance and help of the woodwork teacher at St. Paul's Comprehensive School. After Mass there were refreshments and a lot of memories with log books and old photos on display.

Other activities during the year included an indoor camp fire and a health education lecture on drugs and a debate on drink driving. Targets had been set at the beginning of the year, one of them being which patrol could travel the furthest distance in the month of January using as many modes of transport as possible. February's challenge was to see which patrol could recruit the most new members. We had a sponsored litter pick up to raise funds for a campaign advertised in the Lincolnshire Echo to bring a burns victim, Gabriella Mazzali, from Australia following a terrible accident in which she had received near fatal burns. Her home was near our head quarters in Brant Road. The scouts collected £70 for the fund.

We held a leaders training camp. One hadn't been run for years. Nine leaders attended, the group scout leader, five cub and beaver leaders and three scout leaders. The programme was organised along the lines of a typical Scout camp. Skill sessions were run dealing with rope work, erecting a tent, use of hand axe and saw, health and safety and camp inspections.

There was some misapprehension by those who did not do much camping especially in the Cub and Beaver sections. We were able to demonstrate that although you don't have all the creature comforts that you have at home, a good camper has no need to rough it. The emphasis as on fun, friendship and teamwork. We had a good time and decided to make it an annual event.

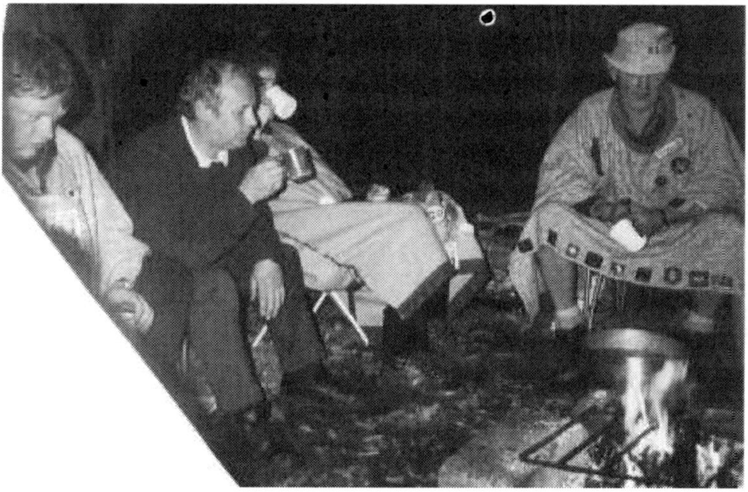

Leaders Training Camp October 1994
From left: John, Keith, Phillip, the author in cap fire blanket

Aletha Beaver Leader at the Leaders Training Camp in 1994

In 1994, a code of conduct was published which stated, 'that it is the policy of the Scout movement to safeguard the welfare of its members by protecting them from physical, sexual and emotional harm.'

It was a constant challenge for leaders to come up with new ideas and challenges when compiling the troop programme. We kicked off in 1995 with debates on euthanasia and alcohol misuse. We held a computer night and had a ju-jitsu demonstration. This was followed by patrol leaders and assistant patrol leaders' winter camp and a group cross country run across South common.

A survival camp was held in July for the older scouts which included the bulk of the patrol leaders and assistant patrol leaders. The scouts had to build a bivouac and sleep in it, know how to skin a rabbit and purify water, cook without utensils and boil water in a paper bag. They also had to take part in an incident hike which involved finding casualties, dealing with their injuries and constructing stretchers to transport them to safety.

Summer camp was held at Drum Hill in Derbyshire. As we had camped there before I will just recount the one incident. The leaders were sleeping in a small marquee when I was woken by something lying on top of me. I realised that the tent had collapsed. I tumbled out of my warm sleeping bag and out into the cold, wet, misty morning, half asleep and throwing on some clothes as I went. The sight that met me was one of confusion with leaders in various states of undress scurrying hither and thither and muttering a few expletives. Close by stood a herd of cows watching our antics with interest. It was obvious what had happened. The cows had caught their horns on the guy ropes, taking them with them when they moved on causing the whole lot to fall on top of us. It seemed that someone had left a gate open which had let the cows in. Fortunately nobody was injured, only our pride. It could have been a different story if one of the beams, which were pretty solid, had come down on our heads.

A disgraceful incident took place in October when two of our young leaders, Phillip Moore and Peter Moore, (they were not related) were attacked outside the scout headquarters by a gang of six thugs. Phillip managed to break free and phone the police. In the meantime, Peter was hit from behind with an iron bar. He spent six hours in casualty and had several stitches in his scalp. Peter was a diabetic and an epileptic sufferer. Later that night, he was admitted to hospital, mainly as a result of the attack and spent several days there. The youths were arrested and charged with G.B.H. (Grievous Bodily Harm). It was an unprovoked attack on two committed leaders, one of them a Queen's Scout.

We had had incidents of crowds of teenage boys and girls collecting outside the Church centre on Scout nights, banging on the windows and peering through the doors, trying to disrupt the meeting. We had had to go out and talk to drunken youths and ask them to go away and behave and we had several instances when our outside store was broken into and equipment either damaged or stolen.

Activities that year included a visit to Lincoln City Football Club, a debate on whether boxing should be banned, a fancy dress night and basic pioneering and cooking nights. Challenges included having to design a recruitment poster. These were then printed off and distributed in doctors' waiting rooms, local shops and the Church Centre. The posters had slogans like, 'Why not come and give us a try,' and, 'It's education made fun and it's great for children.'

Other challenges included seeing who could raise the most money for charity and which patrol organised the most events.

It was Poacher time again, my third. This time the theme was periods in history;- the 60s, Arthurian, Saxon, Elizabethan, Roundheads and Cavaliers. The two 28th troops were Victorians. My dress was cloth cap, waistcoat, plus fours, long socks, tweed jacket, boots and, to finish off, a drooping moustache.

Our sub group comprised scouts and guides from Sweden and Norway. Sainsbury was the main sponsor of the camp but we were also supported by Morrisons, Lincoln College of Agriculture, Ciba and Wilkinsons.

New activities were American line dancing, Morris dancing, Spirit of England, mock battles and displays, Wild West Gold Rush and International tea parties organised by the Japanese guides. Something else new was that each camp was asked to submit a collage showing some aspect of the area in which we lived in Victorian times.

March 1996 was a very sad time for the troop and the group. My assistant leader, Phillip Moore died age 23 years. He was well known throughout the area and always ready to lend a hand within the group. Diabetes and epilepsy had caused his death. His Resurrection Mass was attended by family, friends and colleagues from the scouting world. The Church, St Peters and St Pauls where he had been a parishioner was packed to capacity. I, as the scout leader and family friend, having known Phillip since his cub days, was given the daunting but privileged task of delivering the Panegyric. The Communion hymn was the well known Scout one, Kum-by-Yah. A guard of honour made up of cubs, scouts, guides and leaders lined the route into the Church. Phillip was dressed in his scout uniform and his coffin was draped in the Union Jack and the Scout flag. At the grave side the Scout hymn was sung, 'Rest in peace, brother Scout.'

There was a light moment on a very, very sad day when Phillip's youngest brother, Matthew who was five years old, turned to his father as we were walking towards the grave in a sombre mood and said, "Dad, I know Phillip has to be buried but do we have to dig the hole?"

Phillip will be sorely missed. He had been in the Scout movement for fifteen years but his memory will live on. His father (Malcolm) was and, in fact, still is an Assistant District Commissioner and his mother a Beaver leader. At the time, he had one brother in the Cubs, another in the Beavers and one in the Scouts. I had received all four brothers into the troop.

The cover if the Gang Show 1996

Soon after this, we welcomed two more leaders into the group, Tina and Ian Shaw.

Saxon Cubs came fourth in the District Cross country run in the under nines and third in the over nines out of 25 cub packs taking part.

The 28th expanded further with a Crusader Venture Unit being formed. Twelve members attended the first meeting. Ros Gizzard, the Venture Scout Leader had three very able assistants. The Vikings, the Thursday group had been restarted after a short break with Dave Spinks as leader and Angela Riggall as Assistant Scout Leader. Three cubs came up to start the troop and within three weeks there were nine new members. Another new development saw the Viking cubs taking girls and the first new members were invested.

A special camp called a Battle Camp was devised and organised by Richard Moore, one of our patrol leaders. It was a type of wide game played over a 24 hour period. Some 35 Scouts from both troops took part. It started on Saturday morning and went right through until 10a.m. on Sunday morning with brief breaks for rest and meals. Despite my initial concerns, the camp was a great success and the immediate comment was, 'When is the next one?'

The Gang Show that year was dedicated to the memory of Phillip Moore.

The second half of the year included activities like Flags and their History, a wide game at Hartsholme Country Park, a disco run by the patrol leaders, inviting the Waddingtom Scouts and Guides to visit and training for the pioneering and hikers badge.

We started 1997 with a coming up ceremony, award of badges and a trophy for the best patrol of 1996. A night hike was held with Waddington Scouts in February and a Patrol leaders and assistant patrol leaders' camp was held at Walesby forest. The proficiency badge of the month was the Ambulance badge. There were sessions on backwood cooking and a district canoe race – we didn't win anything but we acquitted ourselves well. We also took part in the District Sports day and finished amongst the top six troops with some individual successes.

28th Lincoln (Saxon) Troop in 1997
Leaders are: Tim Gates ASL, Bosun S/L, Laura Brown A/SL

Lord Crawshaw, the County Commissioner for Leicestershire, died aged 64 years old. The 4th Lord Crawshaw was a remarkable man who had been confined to a wheel chair since he was 19, following a riding accident. I met his Lordship on several occasions, the most memorable being when he opened our new headquarters in 1965 and we carried his wheelchair with him from his car into the Scout room. He never gave in to his affliction although he suffered a lot of pain. He led a full life and was an inspiration to all who met him and a good role model to young people.

We introduced observation as an activity which is all about getting the Scouts to notice what is going on around them. If we were in the countryside, they were taught to look out for distant landmarks such as hills, churches, towers, rivers and lakes or nearer landmarks like houses, trees, gates and fences which would help them navigate around the area. It is just as important to notice things in an urban setting as well as in a rural one.

One of the exercises we did was called Kim's game where you placed a number of articles on a tray and covered them over. The Scouts were then informed that they had two minutes to look at them when the cover was removed and they were not to ask any questions. The items would be covered again and the Scouts would be expected to write down what they had seen. Most Scouts would barely remember half of the items but, with practice, their memories improved. They were taught not to try and remember every single item but to group them together, for example, if there were pens, pencils and envelopes, then think stationery. By doing that, they could remember the groups more easily than the single items and then break down those groups.

A further observation exercise was to take a group along the High Street, asking them to notice the shops, buildings and people. At the end of the walk, we would ask them questions like, 'What was the name of the jewellers?' or, 'How much was the track suit in Burton's window?' It was training to get the scouts to not only look straight ahead but at the periphery of their vision, noting what was going on above and beneath them as well around them. Most people tend to look straight ahead – tunnel vision – and see nothing unless it is straight in front of them.

One interesting exercise was to ask someone they didn't know or was disguised, to come into the room and take a number of objects, then leave. The scouts were then asked to give a description of the stranger so that he could be reported to the police. It was amazing how many of the scouts would not even have noticed the stranger let alone been able to give a description of him. They were taught first of all to notice the stranger's height, colour of hair, facial features, how they were dressed and what they said.

Scouts weren't taught to only use their sight, they were expected to use their other senses, touch, hearing and smell. We used a game called, 'Silent Indian,' to test their hearing. One scout would be blindfolded. He would have a bunch of keys under his chair and some bean bags in his lap. Starting from the other end of the room, scouts took it in turn to climb over a number of obstacles and seize the keys without being hit by a bean bag which the sentry would throw when he heard a noise. The game had to be carried out in absolute silence so that the sentry had a chance to hear.

We placed a number of bottles for the smell exercise under the noses of the blindfolded scouts who would have to say what was in them having identified the smells. Then they would write down their answers.

The touch exercise was a firm favourite. This was where various objects were placed in envelopes, numbered and hung up on a line. The scouts had to feel the envelopes and say what was in them.

Special games nights were always popular when a selection of the most enjoyable games were played. The one they liked best was Hopping Jenny, Port and Starboard, Spin the plate, Uni-hoc, Cat fighting, Dog and the bone and Silent Indian.

I was informed on 10 March 1997 that the Chief Scouts had awarded me the Medal of Merit which was presented to me by the County Commissioner, Alan Scott, in July 1997.

For the 1997 Battle Camp, the theme was Israelis and the P.L.O. along with the United Nations. The idea of the camp was again one devised by the patrol leaders. There was a set amount of points that each team could win after completing one of the set tasks. Both the Israelis and the P.L.O. could be caught by the U.N. (who were the leaders) but only on each other's territory, not on their own. Each side could catch the other side's leader by tagging him twice in ten seconds. Once an individual was tagged, he would be escorted back to the enemy's base to sign that team's chart. Each side could seize the others flag simply by snatching it and running back to their own base with it. It all sounds complicated but it was good fun and it was a game the scouts had devised and managed themselves.

This two day event cost £10 for food, transport and camping fee. The added bonus was that the weather stayed fine. I can't remember which side won or, as often happens in real life, if it was stalemate.

Before the end of the year, we held an 'On Parade in 1908' night which included some old fashioned quarter staff drill, estimation – height, width and distance, semaphore, fall in parade style, tallest right, shortest left. We also played Victorian games such as blindfold boxing and dog and a bone. We finished off the evening with an old Scout song, 'I've got that B.P. feeling in my heart to stay.'

Sandra Horsefield, a new leader, joined our group in November. In the same month, Fox patrol received a certificate for taking part in, 'Operation Goodwill,' collecting dozens of tins of food for charity.

A training day was held at R.A.F. Cranwell for the Fireman's badge and, in the same month, a patrol leaders camp was held for both troops in Walesby Forest. The camp was organised by our Senior P.L., Richard Dainty. The programme included a skills assault course, a hike to Clumber Park and a debate on capital punishment as well as first aid training.

In April, Aimee Roberts photo was featured on the front page of the Trader with her escort. She was carrying the troop flag at the St George's day parade. Aimee was one of our Chief Scout award winners. The following month, Aimee was at the Chief Scout's Award Ceremony and had her picture taken with the County Commissioner, Alan Scott.

A district camp was held in May, a pirate camp. The three pirate captains were Hook, Pugwash and Blood. They were the camp organisers. Other leaders and helpers were privateers. The Venture Scouts were Freebooters, the scouts were Corsairs and the cubs, Bucaneers while the Beavers were Picaroons. The plot was that Captain Flint's booty was hoarded away and it was a test to see which was the first group to find it. The various parties had to gain tokens to find the hidden clues. It was a good, old fashioned wide game. Other characters were thrown in, Blind Pugh, Bones, Ben Gunn and Calico Kate. It was all good fun even if the plot was a bit convoluted.

Two Scouts, Craig Percival and David Gault organised a nine mile hike with a two night stop over at Laughterton. It was their first attempt at organising such an event. 15 scouts attended and it was an unmitigated success.

The summer camp was held at Bently Copse, a headquarter site in Surrey.

Four of our scouts, Craig Percival, Simon Gates, Aimee Holland and Laura Colindale undertook the three day expedition for the Chief Scouts challenge.

I wrote to the Sunday Times in 1999 about the article they had printed about Scouting in which they were suggesting that it was in deep trouble owing to its declining popularity and was one of the last casualties of the twentieth century, still trading on the ideals of the nineteenth. The article had continued, 'Looking back, it is hard to see when the rot set in but it must have been the swinging sixties. Scouts are simply naff, a survival from an empire that modern, middle class kids don't even get taught about in school.'

In my reply, I pointed out the Scouting is the biggest, uniformed, youth movement in the world with in excess of 25 million members. It is the largest mixed youth movement in the United Kingdom having half a million youngsters taking part in scouting week after week. Further comments on my part suggested that, instead of knocking the Scout movement which appears to be the norm in the so called modern and trendy sections of the media, T.V. or press, I would like to see some recognition of the good work carried out by the thousands of leaders and young people who freely give of their time up and down the country, year in and year out.

I ended by saying that while Scouting would not appeal to every youngster, the movement would continue to appeal to a sufficient number to keep it going for the next hundred years despite counter attractions and past-times that compete for young people's attention.

We were informed in the Lad's Magazine in February, 1999 that Neil Holmes had died unexpectedly. He was the Assistant Scout Leader with the 28th Viking troop. His wife and family are also involved in Scouting. They can rely on our support in their time of grief. May he rest in peace.

Four new leaders joined us, also in February, Julie Finn, Cherie Hardwick, Sharon Harrison and Denise Bailey.

I took the decision to resign from the troop when we returned from our summer camp at Drum hill in Derbyshire. This was partly for family reasons and partly because I had to. I had had a good innings, 44 years, and a younger leader was needed. I was in the fortunate position of having an extremely capable assistant leader, Tim Gates, who had been with the group for a number of years and there were also several young leaders (such as Vasos Milides, Stuart Brown and Vernon Lloyd and Laura Brown who had all come up through the ranks) who would give him every support so the troop would be in capable hands. I wouldn't leave without regret that my Scouting career had come to an end but I also had a feel good factor. I had achieved something worthwhile in my life and the memory of my scouting days would remain with me for the rest of my life.

Myself and Mary, my wife on the presentation of my leaving the 28th, with Tim Gates

My last troop meeting was on Friday, October the 9th 1999. All the scouts, cubs, beavers and leaders assembled and my wife was presented with a beautiful bouquet of flowers and I was given a bottle of brandy and some vouchers. There were refreshments and a lovely cake had been made with the Scout badge on it and my scout name, Bosun. It was a wonderful but sad evening. Both Mary and I were grateful at the send off. But the troop hadn't finished with me and asked me to make sure that I attended Scout Church parade on the 10th of October. I was asked to do a reading at the service and, in the presence of the Group Scout Leader and the County Commissioner, I was thanked for my past service to the troop, group and district and Scouting in general. I found it a very humbling experience.

Final Group gathering to say goodbye to me

In December, I replied to an article in the Times called, 'Let's hear it from the Scouts.' The article knocked the movement and speculated about the horror stories regarding child molestation and the fact that there had been three of these cases each year since 1995 and that, therefore, there must be many more that haven't been reported.

In my reply, I acknowledged that one such case was one too many but that the Scout movement had an excellent record on child protection issues, especially when you compared ours to those of children's homes and abuse by step parents and other family members. Abuse is rare in Scouting but when it does occur, it hits the headlines because it's rare. It is a fact that due to the very nature of its involvement with young people, it does attract some unsavoury characters. While stringent checks are made, it is inevitable that some cases slip through the net.

I negotiated with the troop to join the Poacher camp 2000 and be with them one last time. Perhaps I should explain the history of the Poacher. The idea was conceived in 1973 that an International Scout and Guide camp would take place in 1977. The event was to be jointly organised by the Scout and Guide movements. Around 4,000 scouts and guides attended the first Poacher and, because of its success, a similar camp has been run every five years until 1992 when a decision was made to run them every four years to coincide with the millennium. The theme of 2000 was planets and the six sub groups were Buck Rogers, Red Dwarf, Dr Who, Star Trek, Star Wars and Superman. Our group was Dr Who. The camp, as usual was full of hustle and bustle. The programme included fencing, clay pigeon shooting, Aerial runway, simulator, quad bikes and a climbing tower. Entertainment was provided by roller discos, a gospel group, circus tricks, a murder evening, talent contests, an evening of magic and an international tea party. One of the highlights was the visit of the Chief Scout, George Purdy and the Chief Guide, Bridget Towle.

I attended a camp fire run by our sub group and was volunteered by the scouts for a sketch which the guides had organised. They had built a tardis and were seeking volunteers in order to demonstrate how many people could enter it. Several people had already entered, obviously through the front and exited by the back. So far, so good, it was completely harmless. My fate was to be different but I was completely unaware of that at the time. When I went in, the box on which it stood was rolled down the slope and I was left to stew inside until they released me, unharmed but with my dignity ruffled.

The highlight for me was being asked by the Group scout leader, Linda Wilson, to invest two scouts in front of both our troops. I have carried out hundreds of investitures over the years and every one has been special but this one was doubly so being held on the County showground. It is one I will always treasure.

The Poacher prayer at the end of the camp was, “Lord we thank you for bringing us together to share this camp with our friends. Each new day we celebrate that we have our strengths, our talents, our labours, our peace, our joy, our fun. In all challenges and activities of Poacher, help us to find time to think of you wherever we go, in whatever we do and at the end of the day give us peace in our hearts.”

With the end of Poacher 2000 came the end of my Scouting career which had spanned four and a half decades. There was a tinge of sorrow but I was going in the knowledge that, if given the chance, I would have undertaken another 44 years. B.P. said in his last message, “Try to leave this world a better place than you found it and, when your turn comes to die, you can die happily feeling that, at any rate, you haven’t wasted your time but have done your best. Be prepared to live happy and die happy, stick to your Scout promise always even after you have ceased to be a boy and, God help you to do it.”

Although I left the Scout movement in 2000, I couldn't resist the chance of visiting Poacher 2004. Through the auspices of Angela Riggall, one of my ex-assistant leaders who is also an Assistant Commissioner in Lincoln, I obtained a day pass to visit the camp.

I reported to the Security Checkpoint at 9.30am at the County Show Group (which is situated some three miles outside of Lincoln) and received my pass which also contained my photo and commenced to explore the Camp Site. Once I worked out where the foreign contingents were located I sought out Scouts, Guides and leaders to swop badges, waddles, neckerchiefs and other scouting memorabilia. I spent several hours in this pursuit talking with Americans, Canadians, Japanese and Indian groups, among others. I also wandered around taking photos of the various sites that caught my eye and sampled some of the hospitality and refreshments on offer. After all, "A scout is a friend to all and a brother to every other scout no matter what country, class or creed the other may belong."

Other highlights of the day were seeing the chief Scout George Purdy having a go on the climbing wall, attending a swopping session in the International tent and visiting my old scout troop the 28th Lincoln. The 28th made me feel very welcome and it was great to reminisce about old times. However, it was all too soon to take my leave and as I handed in my pass, I dwelt upon my many happy memories of the day and the souvenirs I had acquired. Yes, it was certainly a memorable day that I will long remember.

Grantham Division Camp,
Poacher 2004

The chief Scout George Purdy at the Poacher 2004 International Camp with four Japanese Guides

Danish Camp Site Poacher 2004

Climbing Tower
Poacher 2004

Waddington Scout Camp, Poacher 2004

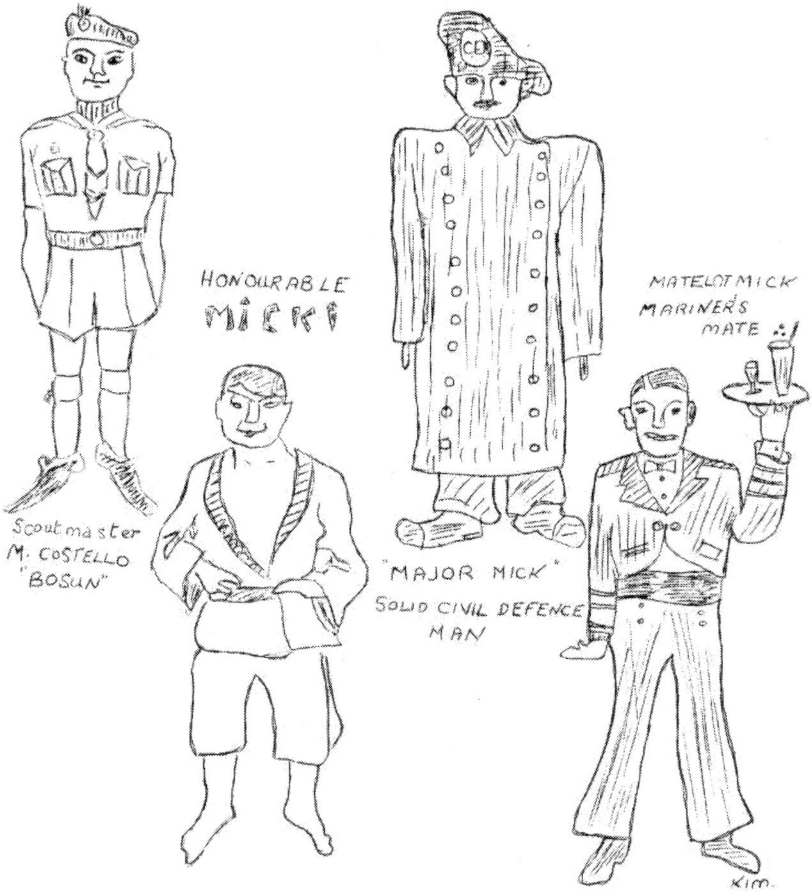

Sketches done by Scouts of the 74th Leicester in 1964 depicting the author in various roles of Scouter, Civil Defence worker, Ju-Jitsu instructor and waiter in the Merchant Navy. Taken from the Troop Magazine 'Maroon and White'.

A good Scout leaves nothing behind but his thanks and I thank God for allowing me the time to have belonged to the worldwide brotherhood of Scouting.

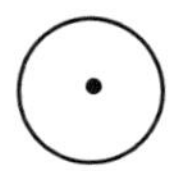

(This means it is ended, I have gone home)

Facts & Figures

Did you know.........?

By 1966 it was estimated that some 3,000,000 men in the UK had been Scouts, some 15% of the male population.

One boy in nine between the ages of 8 and 18 was a scout.

Former Scouts and Guides included: Harold Wilson, Stirling Moss, Ken Dodd, Sir Gerald Templer, King George VI, Cliff Richard, Kate Moss, Carol Vorderman, Keith Richards and Paul McCartney.

The United States has the largest number of Scouts in the world today (2007) with 10 million and Indonesia and India each have some 8 ½ million scouts.

In 1910, 10,500 boy scouts and a fair number of girls gathered at Crystal Palace for the first ever Scout Rally.

Baden-Powell wrote 32 books and was a prolific painter.

AWARDS AND DECORATIONS

The Scout movement has a range of awards and decorations to recognise loyalty, service, courage and heroic actions. The highest award is the Cornwall Badge, or Scout V.C. as it is commonly known

Cornwall Badge	Scout V.C.
Silver Cross	Heroic Action
Gilt Cross	Great Courage
Silver Wolf	Service of the most exceptional character over many years
Silver Acorn	Special Distinguished service
Medal for Meritorious Conduct	Great courage and Enthusiasm
Bar to Medal of Merit	In recognition of further Outstanding Service
Medal of Merit	In recognition of Outstanding Service
Chief Scouts Award for Meritorious Conduct	In recognition of Calm Action
Certificate for Meritorious Conduct	Great Courage and Dedication to Scouting
Bar to Long Service Award	25 Years Service
Long Service Award	15 Years Service
Thanks Badge	for Lay Helpers

Glossary

PL	Patrol Leader
A/PL	Assistant Patrol Leader
S/PL	Senior Patrol Leader
S/L	Scout Leader
ASL	Assistant Scout Leader
GSL	Group Scout Leader
VS	Venture Scout
VSL	Venture Scout Leader
AVSL	Assistant Venture Scout Leader
CL	Cub Leader
ACL	Assistant Cub Leader
DC	District Commissioner
CC	County Commissioner

Bibliography

Scouting for Boys	BP
Scouting around the World	JS Wilson
The Chief Scout	WJ Batchelder
The Way to Camp	SH Walker (1949)
Norfolk Scout Song Book	Norwich Scout Shop (1950)
Maroon & White	MAG 64th Leicester
Lads	MAG 28th Lincoln
Catholics & Scouting	Rev Patrick W Corigan